for the Southern armies. General-in-Chief Henry W. Halleck forcefully emphasized the strategic value of the Mississippi in a dispatch to Maj. Gen. Ulysses S. Grant on March 20, 1863, as Grant prepared to launch his final Vicksburg offensive. "The great objective on your line now is the opening of the Mississippi River, and everything else must tend to that purpose. The eyes and hopes of the whole country are now directed to your army. In my opinion, the opening of the Mississippi River will be to us of more advantage than the capture of forty Richmonds."

Equally determined to protect this vital lifeline, the Confederates erected a series of fortifications at readily defensible points along the river from below New Orleans to Columbus, Kentucky, from which Federal movements could be checked. But Union army and navy units, pushing southward from Illinois and northward from the Gulf of Mexico by land and water, attacked the Confederate strongholds from both ends of the line, capturing post after post and city after city until, by late spring of 1862, only Vicksburg posed a major obstacle to total Union possession of the Mississippi.

Protected by heavy artillery batteries on the riverfront and with land approaches to the north guarded by densely wooded swamplands, Vicksburg defied large-scale land and river expeditions for more than a year. The North's efforts to capture and the South's efforts to defend this mighty river fortress during 1862-63 resulted in what one of the city's defenders, Gen. Stephen D. Lee, called "the most decisive and far-reaching battle of the war." "Here at Vicksburg," said Lee, "over one hundred thousand gallant soldiers and a powerful fleet of gunboats and ironclads in terrible earnestness…fought to decide whether the new Confederate States should be cut in twain; whether the great river should flow free to the Gulf, or should have its commerce hindered.

The photograph shows one of the well-protected Confederate river batteries that defended Vicksburg. Located about 200 yards from the Mississippi River and virtually impregnable to direct assault, it was ideally situated for the defense of the city. The photograph was made soon after Pemberton's surrender. The tents in the background show a Union encampment that occupied the position after Vicksburg fell.

Queen City of the Bluffs

A busy river town with a thriving steamboat and railroad trade, Vicksburg perched on a line of bluffs overlooking a sweeping horseshoe bend in the Mississippi. Residents called it "the queen city of the bluffs." Young Lucy McRae, a local diarist, thought of it in 1860 as a place of "culture, education and luxury."

With good reason, for the town's 4,500 inhabitants, supported scores of trades, shops, and businesses: druggists, tailors, dressmakers, bakers, lawyers, gunsmiths, jewelers, publishers, bookbinders, whiskey dealers, carriage-makers, gambling houses, confectioners, and stove-makers. The courthouse, built in 1858 on one of the highest hills in Vicksburg, symbolized the city's growing importance. It was a local landmark and during the war became a ranging point for Union guns. The cupola was used by Confederate soldiers as a signal station. Militarily, Vicksburg was a strategic prize and might have been taken by almost any Union force that reached it during the first year of the war when the garrison was small and its fortifications barely begun. By the summer of 1862, however, it had become the Confederacy's strongest remaining citadel on the Mississippi. Its artillery on the bluffs shut off Union river traffic from the Gulf, denying the Midwest a market for its agricultural surplus. While it stood,

Vicksburg gave the South a vital rail and river link to its own cattle, hog, and hominy region of Louisiana, Texas, and Arkansas, and a focal point for Confederate resistance. The engraving below shows the city in wartime with the courthouse (center) and the spires of several churches rising in the background. The photo at left shows the "Widow Blakely," a British-made rifled cannon that helped guard the riverfront south of Vicksburg against Union warships.

President Abraham Lincoln, knew well Vicksburg's value to the South. "We may take all the northern ports of the Confederacy," he said, "and they can still defy us from Vicksburg. It means hog and hominy without limit, fresh troops from all the states of the far South, and a cotton country where they can raise the staple without interference."

Lincoln's views were shared by Maj. Gen. Ulysses S. Grant, who considered the city's capture "a matter of the first importance…equal to the amputation of a limb in its weakening effects upon the enemy."

David G. Farragut, commanding the West Gulf Blockading Squadron, headed the Union's first attempt to take Vicksburg during the late spring and early summer of 1862. He had already stunned the South by capturing New Orleans. Although forced to abandon his Vicksburg operations, Farragut's earlier successes brought him promotion to admiral, the U. S. Navy's first.

Naval commander Charles H. Davis led the Western Gunboat Flotilla and forced the surrender of Memphis, then joined Farragut for the attack on Vicksburg.

Maj. Gen. William T. Sherman, XV Corps commander, initially distrusted Grant's final plan for capturing Vicksburg, thinking it "desperate and hazardous." "I feel in its success less confidence than in any similar undertaking of the war," he wrote his brother, "but it is my duty to cooperate with zeal and I shall endeavor to do it." Later, Sherman applauded the plan's brilliance, calling the result "the first gleam of daylight in the war."

Flag Officer Andrew Hull Foote, a naval commander who enjoyed early successes. Foote led the Western Gunboat Flotilla against Confederate strongholds on the lower Mississippi, Cumberland, and Tennessee Rivers until an old battle wound impaired his health and he relinquished command to Davis.

Confederate Leaders in the Vicksburg Campaign

Confederate President Jefferson Davis, viewed Vicksburg as "the nailhead that held the South's two halves together" and told his commander there, John C. Pemberton that it "must be saved." Many Southerners distrusted the Northern-born Pemberton, but Davis' support never faltered.

Lt. Gen. John C. Pemberton. commander of the Confederate army that defended Vicksburg against the Federal onslaught. "I selected General Pemberton for the very important command which he now holds," Davis told an associate, "from a conviction that he was the best qualified officer for that post then available, and I have…found no reason to change the opinion…."

Gen. Joseph Eggleston Johnston, commanding the Confederate Departments of Tennessee and Mississippi, impressed people as "a perfect specimen of a soldier" and inspired great devotion among the men he led, even in defeat. He and Pemberton "differed widely" over how best to defend Vicksburg, Johnston favoring movement and mobility to Pemberton's preference for fortifications and fixed positions. It was a difference that affected not only their professional relations but the fate of Vicksburg as well.

Maj. Gen. John S. Bowen tried to stop Grant's army at Port Gibson. Though his outnumbered Confederate brigades fought stubbornly, his limited strength "made victory for him impossible" and he was forced to withdraw. He fought again at Champion Hill and commanded the Confederate reserve division during the Vicksburg siege.

Col. Edward Higgins commanded the Confederate river batteries at Vicksburg. It was his job to defend the city against attacks by and landing attempts from the Federal gunboats on the Mississippi.

Maj. Gen. Carter L. Stevenson, above, who was transferred from Braxton Bragg's Army of Tennessee and led his division at Champion Hill.

11

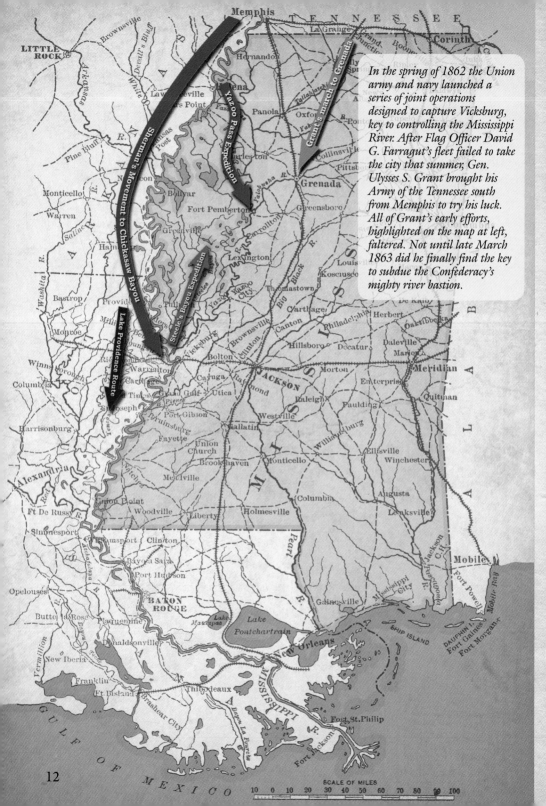

In the spring of 1862 the Union army and navy launched a series of joint operations designed to capture Vicksburg, key to controlling the Mississippi River. After Flag Officer David G. Farragut's fleet failed to take the city that summer, Gen. Ulysses S. Grant brought his Army of the Tennessee south from Memphis to try his luck. All of Grant's early efforts, highlighted on the map at left, faltered. Not until late March 1863 did he finally find the key to subdue the Confederacy's mighty river bastion.

SCALE OF MILES
10   0   10   20   30   40   50   60   70   80   90   100

The Campaign

Vicksburg sat on a hairpin bend of the Mississippi on bluffs that rose abruptly several hundred feet above the water – the first high ground on the east side of the river below Memphis and the only rail and river junction between Memphis and New Orleans. A railroad running east from the city connected with others leading to every significant point in the South; across the river another railroad ran west to Monroe, Louisiana. Through the city much of the supplies from the Trans-Mississippi were shipped to Confederate forces in the East. Artillery frowned from the crest, slope, and base of the bluffs. Confederate President Jefferson Davis considered Vicksburg "the Gibraltar of America;" President Abraham Lincoln called it the "key" to Union victory, and believed that the war could not be brought to a successful conclusion "until that key is in our pocket."

The first attempt to put the Vicksburg key in Lincoln's pocket began in April 1862, when Flag Officer David G. Farragut headed his West Gulf Blockading Squadron of ocean-going vessels up the Mississippi and captured New Orleans, the South's largest city. A small Federal flotilla proceeded 400 miles farther upriver and received the surrenders of Baton Rouge, capital of Louisiana, and Natchez, Mississippi. These ships arrived just below Vicksburg on May 18, and were subsequently joined by the remainder of Farragut's fleet.

During Farragut's 1862 attack on Vicksburg each of Porter's mortar boats carried one of these giant 17,000-pound mortars which hurled 200-pound shells into the city.

Meantime, Flag Officer Andrew H. Foote's Western Flotilla had moved down the Mississippi from Cairo, Illinois, providing support to the army in reducing Confederate river strongholds. The striking power of this so-called "Inland Navy" was largely provided by nine ironclad gunboats, including seven "Pook Turtles" mounting 13 guns each in partially armored casemates, and Col. Charles Ellet's ram fleet. (Foote, incapacitated by combat wounds, was replaced early in May by Flag Officer Charles H. Davis.) After capturing Memphis in early June and destroying the Confederate upriver fleet of converted river steamboats, the Federal vessels pushed southward and on July 1 dropped anchor beside a portion of Farragut's fleet just north of Vicksburg. All of the Mississippi River was now in Union hands, except for the section commanded by the Vicksburg batteries.

These batteries were passed for the first time on June 28, when two sloops of war and six gunboats fought their way upriver. On that day, in an attempt to reduce the city by naval attack, Farragut blasted Vicksburg and its defenses with broadsides from his ships and a devastating fire from Cmdr. David D. Porter's mortar schooners. The attempt failed, making it clear that a powerful land force would be required to capture "Fortress" Vicksburg. Only 3,000 infantry had accompanied the expedition, and they were put to work with pick and shovel to dig a cutoff, southwest of the city, which might permit river traffic to bypass the Vicksburg guns.

Farragut now realized that he would have to withdraw from the city. The hot, fetid atmosphere of the river increased the disease rate to such an extent that only 800 of the 3,000 soldiers were fit for duty. At the same time, the steadily falling waters threatened to maroon his deep-draught vessels. By late July Farragut's warships and troop transports returned to Baton Rouge and New Orleans, while Davis steamed upriver, leaving Vicksburg unopposed.

After Farragut's and Davis' withdrawal, Confederate communications east and west of the Mississippi, which had been temporarily curtailed, were reestablished. From Vicksburg to Port Hudson, Louisiana, a distance of 250 miles by water, the river was again in Confederate hands. So too was the Red River, which emptied into the Mississippi just above Port Hudson and down which great

Rear Adm. David D. Porter. His Union mortar flotilla did its best to blast Vicksburg into submission during Farragut's 1862 attempt to capture the city. That failure convinced Porter that the place "could only be taken after a long siege by the combined operations of a large military and naval force." Later, as commander of the Mississippi Squadron, Porter played a conspicuous role in the capture of Arkansas Post in January 1863 and in Grant's Vicksburg's operations.

The Confederate ironclad ram Arkansas runs safely through the combined Union fleets of Farragut, Ellet and Davis above Vicksburg, July 15, 1862. U.S. Navy Secretary Gideon Welles called this spectacular feat of Southern daring "the most disreputable naval affair of the war," while a mortified Farragut vowed vengeance. The Arkansas, however, protected by the Vicksburg batteries, withstood all attempts to destroy her and continued to present a formidable threat to Farragut's wooden ships.

stores of food, sugar, and livestock were floated to supply the armies of the Confederacy. The North would also have to close this important supply route.

The task of clearing the Mississippi of Confederate resistance fell to Maj. Gen. Ulysses S. Grant. In October 1862, Grant, who had won the nickname "Unconditional Surrender" at Fort Donelson the previous February and had rallied his army from near defeat at bloody Shiloh in April, assumed command of the Department of the Tennessee with headquarters at Jackson, Tennessee. The same month, Pennsylvania-born Lt. Gen. John C. Pemberton, a West Pointer who had served in the army with Grant in the Mexican War, was placed in command of the Confederate troops defending the Mississippi. His mission: to keep the river and the Southern supply line open. Vicksburg would become the focus of military operations for both commanders.

In November Grant pushed 40,000 troops south from the Tennessee border along the Mississippi Central Railroad in the first full-scale land-based expedition against Vicksburg. A month later Maj. Gen. William T. Sherman, commanding the army's right wing at Memphis proceeded down river with 32,000 men aboard 60 transports. Grant's plan called for his force to tie down the bulk of Pemberton's troops in northern Mississippi long enough for Sherman to attack the Confederate defense lines at the base of the bluffs a few miles north of the city. But the plan went awry on December 20 when Confederate Maj. Gen. Earl Van Dorn slipped behind the Union lines with a striking force of 3,500 cavalry and destroyed Grant's supply depot at Holly Springs. At the same time, another Confederate force under Brig. Gen. Nathan B. Forrest invaded West Tennessee and wreaked havoc on Grant's Mobile & Ohio Railroad supply line. Unwilling to wage a campaign without a base of supply, Grant returned to Memphis.

Scene of Sherman's unsuccessful attack at Chickasaw Bayou, on December 29, 1862.

On December 29, Sherman assaulted at Chickasaw Bayou, five miles northeast of Vicksburg. The land here was a low, swampy shelf lying between the Yazoo River and the bluffs. The few dry corridors over which his infantry could advance were covered by Confederate small-arms and artillery fire from defense positions at the base of the bluffs. The assaults were repulsed, with the Union army losing more than 1,700 men, compared to Confederate casualties of approximately 200. Sherman tersely reported his defeat: "I reached Vicksburg at the time appointed, landed, assaulted, and failed."

Forced to abandon operations, Sherman fell back to the mouth of the Yazoo where, on January 2, 1863, he was superseded in command by Maj. Gen. John A. McClernand. Almost immediately, McClernand decided to attack Arkansas Post (Fort Hindman), a large bastioned earthwork about 50 miles up the Arkansas River from its junction with the Mississippi and manned by about 5,000 troops. He viewed the attack as a way of relieving a growing threat to the Union right flank and rear, for the Confederates were constantly sending armed detachments down the Arkansas to harass Federal shipping on the Mississippi.

The undertaking began on January 4 and by the 10th McClernand's 30,000 troops supported by 50 transports and gunboats under now-Rear Admiral Porter, had the fort under siege. The Southerners surrendered the place the next day after a three-and-one-half hour land and naval attack. Although the capture of Arkansas Post was one of the few successful Federal operations in an otherwise bleak winter, it failed to weaken materially the Confederate hold on the Vicksburg area.

McClernand decided to attack Arkansas Post (Fort Hindman), a large bastioned earthwork about 50 miles up the Arkansas River from its junction with the Mississippi and manned by about 5,000 troops.

By late January, Grant was ready to try again. Federal forces earmarked for operations against Vicksburg had been assembled in camps on the western side of the Mississippi at Young's Point, Milliken's Bend, and Lake Providence, all upriver from Vicksburg. This army, which Grant assumed immediate command of on January 30, numbered about 45,000 men and was divided into three corps under Sherman, Maj. Gen. John A. McClernand, and Maj. Gen. James B. McPherson. (A fourth corps under Maj. Gen. Stephen A. Hurlbut was guarding West Tennessee.) Cooperating with the army was the Mississippi Squadron under now-Acting Rear Admiral Porter consisting of more than 60 vessels, including ironclads, timberclads, tinclads, and auxiliary craft, mounting more than 300 guns and carrying 5,500 men.

A major problem confronting Grant in his operations against Vicksburg, in addition to Pemberton's army, was the topography of the area, which so favored the defense as to render the city almost impregnable to attack. At this time of year, the only dry ground on which an army might maneuver lay east of the bluffs on which Vicksburg had been built. Grant knew this. What he did not know was how he was going to get his troops onto the bluffs in the first place.

The line of bluffs marking the eastern boundary of the Mississippi Valley leaves the river at Memphis, curves in a great 250-mile arc away from the river, and then swings back to reach the river again at Vicksburg. Enclosed between the bluffs and the river is "The Delta" – a strip of land averaging some 60 miles in width, which is now a fertile, well-drained, cotton-growing region. In 1863, except for the natural levees paralleling Deer Creek and a few other streams, it was a swampy bottomland containing numerous rivers and bayous, subject in winter and spring to incessant flooding. It was covered with thick forests and dense undergrowth, a condition which, according to Grant's engineer officer, "renders the country almost impassable in summer, and entirely so, except by boats in winter." This impenetrable bottomland effectively guarded Vicksburg's right flank. Unless the waterways of The Delta could provide a passage to the bluffs, operations against Vicksburg to the north were hopeless.

South of Vicksburg Grant's prospects were equally dismal. After meeting the river at Vicksburg, the bluffs follow the river course closely to the south and were accessible, therefore, to troops from the Mississippi. But the river batteries of the city prevented the passage of transports, meaning that to get below the city troops would have to move through the Louisiana lowlands west of the river. This region was like The Delta north of Vicksburg – flooded bottomlands interspersed with bayous, rivers, lakes, and a few natural levees. It would prove equally obstinate to land movements.

Adding to these topographical difficulties was the fact that Grant was beginning his campaign during the wet season when streams were overflowing and lowlands impassable. The winter of 1862-63 was a period of unusually heavy rains, causing the Mississippi to crest above its banks from December until mid-April. Had Grant reached Vicksburg during the dry season, his problems would have been less formidable.

The problems, however, were not all on the Federal side. Despite the topography that facilitated his defensive mission, Pemberton knew that Vicksburg would be secure only so long as the Confederate army could keep Grant from gaining a foothold on the high ground above or below the city. To prevent such a lodgement, it was necessary for the Southerners to defend a wide front extending 200 miles above and below Vicksburg, at any point along which the Federals might strike. To guard this large area the Confederate commander would have to spread his limited garrison dangerously thin and at the same time retain sufficient troops to protect the city – his primary responsibility. Under such conditions it was essential that Pemberton be kept informed of Federal movements so he could concentrate his troops rapidly. Unfortunately, his cavalry force was inadequate for this mission and he had almost no navy to interfere with or report Union progress through the rivers and bayous.

Union camp at Young's Point, La. It was here in January 1863 on the west bank of the Mississippi south of Milliken's Bend that Grant assembled part of his military forces to begin the final campaign against Vicksburg.

Meanwhile Grant was busy trying to find a way to get his troops into position to move against Vicksburg. The city's location below a horseshoe bend of the river had already suggested one solution to the Federal commander. By digging a canal across the peninsula below Vicksburg and diverting the river through it, unarmored transports could bypass the city batteries and deliver troops safely to the bluffs below. In late January, elements of McClernand's and Sherman's corps, soon to be assisted by dredging machines, began excavating the 1½ mile-long canal. This project, which came to be known as Grant's Canal, continued until early March when a sudden rise in the river flooded the peninsula, driving the troops to the levees and destroying some of the work. The canal was abandoned when the Confederates erected artillery batteries on the bluffs commanding the lower end and axis of the canal.

While the canal work was in progress, McPherson's corps was trying to turn Vicksburg's left flank by passing southward through the Louisiana waterways to reach the bluffs below the city. A canal was cut to provide entrance from the Mississippi into Lake Providence, 75 river miles above Vicksburg. From Lake Providence a route was plotted through the labyrinth of bayous and rivers by which a fleet might debouch from the Red River into the Mississippi 200 miles below the city and, after assisting in the capture of Port Hudson, move on Vicksburg from the south. While presenting great difficulties to navigation, the entire 400 miles would be safe from enemy action. The dredging of shoals and the sawing off of trees far enough below the water to permit passage of the transports proved the most severe obstacles. The effort to clear the Lake Providence route was abandoned when Federal engineers were unable to establish a navigable channel through Bayou Baxter into Bayou Macon south of Lake Providence.

Another attempt to turn Vicksburg's right flank by sending an amphibious force through Yazoo Pass and connecting Delta waterways to the bluffs northeast of the city for a time offered promise of success. The Federals secured access from the Mississippi River into the interior of The Delta by breaching the levee at Yazoo Pass 320 river miles north of Vicksburg. But before gunboats and infantry transports could steam through the entire length of Yazoo Pass, the waterway had to be cleared of trees felled by Confederate axmen. It was over a month before the last transport reached the deeper waters of the Tallahatchie River.

By then Pemberton had been notified of the threat and rushed troops under the command of Maj. Gen. William W. Loring to halt the Union advance. Ninety miles north of Vicksburg, near the confluence of the Tallahatchie and Yalobusha Rivers which form the Yazoo River, they built Fort Pemberton of earth and cotton bales. The land surrounding the fort was flooded, permitting approach by water only. On March 11, Union gunboats began an artillery bombardment and were promptly greeted by a heavy return fire as "Old Blizzards" Loring gained his nickname by pacing the parapet and urging his gunners to "Give them blizzards, boys! Give them blizzards!" Loring's gunners bested the gunboats in every exchange. Despite considerable effort and extreme exertion, Federal infantry units were unable to organize an attack in the flooded bottomlands. Frustrated at every turn, the expedition returned to the Mississippi.

This shows black laborers, who were pressed into the service of the Federals, working on "Grant's Canal" across De Soto Point opposite Vicksburg. Grant started the canal in January 1863 as one of several "experiments" to get his army safely past the Confederate river batteries. By mid-March, however, he recognized the futility of the effort and abandoned it

21

Union army vanguard leaves Milliken's Bend March 31

Battle of the Big Black River Bridge May 17

Siege of Vicksburg May 18 - July 4

Army arrives Hard Times April 28

Union Fleet bombards Grand Gulf April 29

Army crosses Mississippi River at Bruinsburg Apr 30 - May 1

Battle of Port Gibson May 1

22

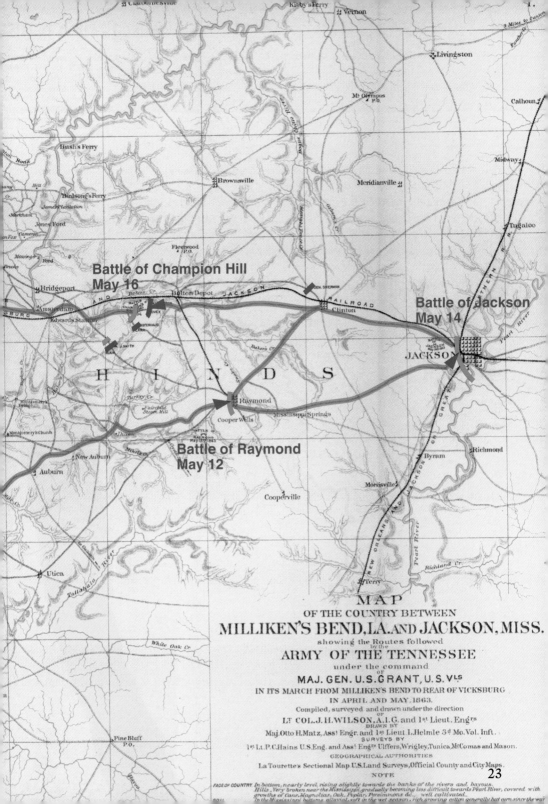

Battle of Champion Hill
May 16

Battle of Jackson
May 14

Battle of Raymond
May 12

MAP
OF THE COUNTRY BETWEEN
MILLIKEN'S BEND, LA. AND JACKSON, MISS.
showing the Routes followed
by the
ARMY OF THE TENNESSEE
under the command
of
MAJ. GEN. U.S. GRANT, U.S. V^{LS}
IN ITS MARCH FROM MILLIKEN'S BEND TO REAR OF VICKSBURG
IN APRIL AND MAY, 1863.
Compiled, surveyed and drawn under the direction
of
L^t COL. J. H. WILSON, A.I.G. and 1st Lieut. Eng^{rs}
DRAWN BY
Maj. Otto H. Matz, Ass^t Engr. and 1st Lieut L. Helmle 3^d Mo. Vol. Inft.
SURVEYS BY
1st Lt. P. C. Hains U.S. Eng. and Ass^t Eng^{rs} Ulffers, Wrigley, Tunica, McComas and Mason.
GEOGRAPHICAL AUTHORITIES
La Tourette's Sectional Map U.S. Land Surveys, Official County and City Maps.
NOTE

23

The last and most extraordinary of the Federals unsuccessful attempts to reach Vicksburg was the Steele's Bayou expedition, which set out in mid-March to follow a 200-mile route through narrow, twisting bayous and rivers north of Vicksburg. Like the Yazoo Pass operation, it was an effort to turn the city's right flank. This shorter route had been originally scouted to send aid to the Yazoo Pass expedition when that force seemed in danger of being cut off and captured. Further exploration suggested the route to the bluffs by way of Steele's Bayou might prove the best of all possible approaches to Vicksburg. Porter himself commanded the squadron comprised of five ironclads, a ram, and four tugs and mortar scows.

The squadron entered the bayou from the Yazoo River on March 14. The route was heavily obstructed by natural hazards, but Porter pushed forward confidently, despite warnings from apprehensive officers that the vessels' superstructures could be carried away in crashing through the closely overhung waterways. "All I need is an engine, guns, and a hull to float them," he told them. Progress was slow through winding streams barely wide enough to admit passage of the gunboats. Alert Confederates nearly succeeded in shutting up and capturing the entire fleet in Deer Creek by felling huge trees to block Porter's retreat.

Sherman, following behind the boats with infantry, received word of Porter's danger, and an eerie night march ensued. By the flaring light of candles held in their hands, the Federal soldiers splashed through the canebrake hip deep in water and arrived in time to drive off the Confederates who had surrounded the Union vessels. The fleet, unable to proceed farther, laboriously made its way back to the Mississippi.

Grant had now tested all possible approaches to Vicksburg as he attempted to swing wide around its flanks to the north and south. Every effort had failed. At the end of March, the Union army was no closer to its objective than it had been in December. The Southern bastion on the Mississippi had successfully withstood Union land and naval attacks for almost a year.

In the eyes of many Northerners, Grant's army had floundered in the swamps around Vicksburg for months with nothing to show for it except a steadily mounting death list from disease. Criticism of the Union commander mounted. "I don't know what to make of Grant, he's such a quiet little fellow," said Lincoln, thinking of the more flamboyant commanders who had led his Eastern armies. "The only way I know he's around is by the way he makes things git." Lincoln had grown increasingly fond of Grant, whose army, while ineffective, had never been inactive. Now he declared to Grant's critics, "I think we'll try him a little longer."

Although Grant had made every effort to navigate the bayous and reach Vicksburg, he entertained little hope of success. But while waiting for the dry season to permit land operations, he had determined to exhaust every possibility and to retain the fighting edge of his army by keeping it constantly on the move. As April approached and the roads began to emerge from the slowly receding waters, Grant prepared to execute the movement which he had believed to be the logical approach against Vicksburg – marching down the west bank of the Mississippi through Louisiana, crossing the river south of the city, and taking it from the rear.

The successful phase of Grant's Vicksburg campaign officially began on March 29, 1863, when he ordered McClernand's corps to open a road for the army from Milliken's Bend to the river below the city. Coincidentally Sherman's troops commenced work on a three-mile long canal connecting the Mississippi River near Duckport Landing (15 river miles above Vicksburg) with Walnut Bayou. Grant believed that a canal from Duckport via Walnut Bayou, Roundaway Bayou, and Bayou Vidal to the river below Vicksburg might offer passage to tugs and supply barges to support the army's march southward. But falling waters defeated the plan.

During April, McClernand's troops labored to bridge streams, corduroy roads, and build flatboats to cross areas still covered by flood waters. During that month also, elements of the Army of the Tennessee accomplished the 70-mile march and assembled at a small hamlet appropriately named Hard Times in view of Grant's unpleasant bayou experiences. Here they were across the river from the Confederate stronghold of Grand Gulf, 60 river miles below Vicksburg.

To ferry the Union army across the Mississippi, it was necessary for a number of the gunboats and transports anchored north of Vicksburg to run the batteries and rendezvous with Grant below the city. Eight gunboats and three transports were designated to run the gauntlet. While naval craft singly and in groups had already successfully passed these batteries on several occasions, it was still a formidable undertaking for which careful preparation was required. As protection against enemy fire the port (left) side of each vessel, which would face the Vicksburg guns in passage, was piled high with bales of cotton and hay. In addition, a coal barge was lashed to the port side of each ironclad and a supply barge to both sides of each transport.

Shortly before midnight, April 16, Confederate pickets in skiffs at the bend of the river above Vicksburg saw the muffled fleet bearing down upon them and gave the alarm. Tar barrels along the bank were ignited and buildings in the small village of De Soto across the river were set afire. The blinding light of a great flare illuminated the river and outlined the fleet for the Confederate gunners. The river batteries thundered at the Union vessels. In return, these boats delivered port broadsides into the city as they passed so close that the clatter of bricks from falling buildings could be heard on board.

Through this "magnificent, but terrible" spectacle – one of the most fearful pageants of the war – steamed the fleet in single file. "Their heavy shot walked right through us," Porter recalled. Every one of the boats was hit, some repeatedly. Several went out of control temporarily, and revolved slowly with the current. Despite the furious bombardment, only one transport was sunk. Within a few days damages were repaired and the fleet soon joined the army at Hard Times Landing. On the night of April 22 six transports, each towing two barges loaded with supplies, ran the batteries with the loss of one transport and six barges.

Union soldiers skirmish in the heavily wooded and flooded bottomlands during the bayou expeditions. The baffling maze of bayous and swamps north of Vicksburg thwarted Grant's efforts to achieve a quick victory and led to demands that he be replaced. Lincoln, however, decided to "try him a little longer."

Grant's plan was to make an assault landing at Grand Gulf, a Confederate stronghold on the bluffs below the mouth of the Big Black River. On April 29 the Union gunboats pounded the Grand Gulf fortifications for 5½ hours in an effort to neutralize the defenses and facilitate the landing of 10,000 Federal infantry aboard transports and barges lying just beyond the range of Confederate cannon. When the naval attack failed to reduce the Confederate works, Grant debarked the troops and marched them southward along the levee to Disharoon's plantation. There they were again met by the gunboats and transports which had slipped downstream under cover of darkness. In a two-day operation, April 30 - May 1, the army crossed the river to Bruinsburg and Grant experienced "a degree of relief scarcely ever equaled since… I was now in the enemy's country, with a vast river and the stronghold of Vicksburg between me and my base of supplies. But I was on dry ground on the same side of the river with the enemy. All the campaigns, labors, hardships, and exposures, from the month of December previous to this time, that had been made and endured, were for the accomplishment of this one object."

Adm. David D. Porter's gunboat flotilla passes the Vicksburg batteries on the night of April 16-17, 1863, to aid Grant's operations below the city. From a Currier & Ives lithograph.

29

The army's landing was unopposed, partly because of Pemberton's decision to hold his troops close to Vicksburg and fight a defensive campaign, and partly because of three diversionary movements that kept the Confederates distracted and helped to screen Grant's true objective. The first of these movements began early in April, when Maj. Gen. Frederick Steele's division of the XV Corps landed at Greenville, 90 miles north of Vicksburg, and, after marching eastward ten miles, advanced south down Deer Creek. To counter this threat to an area from which the Confederate commissary drew most of its "hog and hominy" to feed the Vicksburg garrison, the Confederates rushed a strong column to intercept the Federals. Then on April 17, the day after Porter's running of the batteries underscored for Grant the feasibility of striking from the south, Col. Benjamin H. Grierson with 1,700 cavalrymen rode out from southwestern Tennessee on one of the celebrated cavalry raids of the war. They rode entirely through the state of Mississippi behind Pemberton's army to a junction with Union forces at Baton Rouge, Louisiana. In 16 days Grierson's horsemen covered 476 miles, interfering with Confederate telegraph and railroad communications and forcing Pemberton to march and countermarch infantry and cavalry units to protect his supply and communication lines. Finally, Sherman, whose corps had not yet made the march from Milliken's Bend, made an elaborate feint above Vicksburg. Utilizing a number of the vessels available between Milliken's Bend and the mouth of the Yazoo River, Sherman landed 10 regiments at Blake's lower plantation on the Yazoo north of Vicksburg while Federal gunboats engaged in a lively exchange with Confederate guns emplaced at Drumgould's Bluff.

The events immediately following Grant's landing revealed a basic difference in strategic concepts between Pemberton, commanding the Department of Mississippi and East Louisiana, and Gen. Joseph E. Johnston, his superior officer who was in charge of Confederate operations in Tennessee and Mississippi. Johnston believed that to defeat Grant it would be necessary for Pemberton to unite his forces to smash the Union army, preferably before Grant could consolidate his position on the east bank. Accordingly, he wired Pemberton on May 2: "If Grant's army crosses, unite all your troops to beat him; success will give you back what was abandoned to win it."

Pemberton felt that holding Vicksburg was vital to the Confederacy and that he must primarily protect the city and its approaches. To have marched his army to meet Grant "would have stripped Vicksburg and its essential flank defenses of their garrisons, and the city itself might have fallen an easy prey into the eager hands of the enemy." The inability of Pemberton and Johnston to reach agreement upon the strategy necessary to thwart Grant's invasion seriously hampered subsequent Confederate operations and prevented effective cooperation between the two commanders in the Vicksburg campaign.

Upon debarking on April 30, McClernand's corps headed for the bluffs two miles inland. By late afternoon the Federal soldiers had reached the high ground and pushed on toward Port Gibson, 30 miles south of Vicksburg. Meanwhile, Brig. Gen. John S. Bowen shifted a portion of his Grand Gulf command southeastward to intercept the threat. Early on May 1 leading elements of the Union advance clashed

Major General John A. Logan commanded the 3d Division of James B. McPherson's XVII Corps, which was the first to enter the city of Vicksburg in 1863.

with Bowen's reinforced troops blocking the four roads leading to the town from the south and west.

The battle of Port Gibson was a day-long series of furious clashes over thickly wooded ridges cut by deep, precipitous gullies and covered with dense undergrowth. While greatly outnumbering Bowen, McClernand, though reinforced by one of McPherson's divisions, was prevented by the rugged terrain from bringing his whole force into action. Slowly forced back, Bowen conducted an orderly retreat to Grand Gulf. The holding action had cost Bowen 800 casualties from his command of 8,000. Union losses were slightly higher for a force of 23,000. Two days later Bowen evacuated Grand Gulf and withdrew across the Big Black River. Grant then occupied Grand Gulf, gaining a strong foothold on the east bank of the Mississippi.

McClernand's troops on the march to Port Gibson, where Confederate Gen. John S. Bowen made the first attempt to halt the Federal advance.

Up to the occupation of Grand Gulf, Grant's overall strategy had been first to secure a base on the river below Vicksburg and then to cooperate with Maj. Gen. Nathaniel P. Banks in capturing Port Hudson. After this they planned to move the combined force against Vicksburg. Port Hudson, a strong point on the Mississippi near Baton Rouge, was garrisoned by Confederate troops after Farragut's withdrawal the previous summer. At Grand Gulf, Grant learned that Banks' investment of Port Hudson would be delayed for some time. To follow his original plan would mean postponing his Vicksburg campaign for at least a month, giving Pemberton valuable time to organize his defense and receive reinforcements. This was unacceptable to Grant, who now came to one of the most remarkable decisions of his military career.

Contrary to orders from Washington, Grant decided to move inland against the Confederate force holding Vicksburg, largely subsisting his army from the land through which he marched. The plan was well conceived. By marching to the northeast toward Edwards Station, on the railroad midway between Jackson and Vicksburg, Grant's vulnerable left flank would be protected by the Big Black River. Moreover, his real objective – Vicksburg or Jackson – would not be revealed immediately and could be changed to meet events. By controlling the railroad he would sever Pemberton's communications with Jackson and the East. And while the Confederate forces might outnumber his own, Grant believe that this advantage would be offset by their wide dispersal and by the speed and design of his march.

But this calculated risk was accompanied by grave dangers, of which Grant and his lieutenants were aware. It meant placing the Union army deep in enemy country behind the Confederate army where the line of retreat could be broken and where the alternative to victory would be not only defeat but destruction. The situation was summed up nicely in Sherman's protest, recorded by Grant, "that I was putting myself in a position voluntarily which an enemy would be glad to maneuver a year – or a long time – to get me."

Pemberton's response to the Union threat showed the keenness of Grant's planning. The Confederate general believed that the farther Grant campaigned from the river the weaker his position would become and the more exposed his rear and flanks. Accordingly, Pemberton chose to remain on the defensive, using his army as a shield between Vicksburg and the Union forces and wait for an opportunity to strike a decisive blow – a policy which permitted Grant to march inland unopposed.

On May 7, joined by Sherman's corps from Milliken's Bend, Grant began to march his army to the northeast. His column, totaling 45,000 men, moved in a single avenue much of the way and then spread out on a broad front concealing their objective. To oppose them, Pemberton had about 50,000 available troops, but these were scattered widely to protect important points. His defensive position was further complicated by orders from President Jefferson Davis "to hold both Vicksburg and Port Hudson" because they are "necessary to a connection with the Trans-Mississippi." The Union army, however, was already between Vicksburg and Port Hudson and would soon be between Vicksburg and Jackson.

Compared with campaigns in the more thickly populated Eastern Theater, where a more extensive system of roads and railroads was utilized to provide the tremendous quantities of food and supplies necessary to sustain an army, the operations of Grant's Western veterans ("reg'lar great big, hellsnorters, same breed as ourselves," a charitable "Johnny Reb" called them) represented a new type of warfare. Union supply trains largely consisted of a curious collection of stylish carriages, buggies, and lumbering farm wagons stacked high with ammunition boxes and drawn by whatever mules or horses could be found. Lacking transportation, food supplies were carried in the soldiers' haversacks. Beef, poultry, and pork "requisitioned" from barn and smokehouse enabled the army to largely live off the country.

On April 29 Union gunboats pounded the Grand Gulf fortifications in an effort to neutralize the defenses and facilitate the landing of 10,000 Federal infantry aboard transports and barges lying just beyond the range of Confederate cannon.

Confederate troops charge Logan's division during the Battle of Raymond. Some of the Federals, confused by the dense woods and undergrowth, started to give way but, according to one participant, Logan dashed up "with the shriek of an eagle" and "turned them back to their place, which they regained and held."

When it became likely that Grant's troops would strike the railroad in the vicinity of Edwards Station, Pemberton, leaving behind a strong reserve, moved his main force from the Vicksburg area toward that point. At the same time he ordered Confederate units collecting at Jackson to hit Grant's flank and rear if the opportunity presented itself. Maj. Gen. John A. Logan's division, leading the advance of McPherson's Federal corps, approached within two miles of Raymond, a crossroads town 15 miles southwest of Jackson, on May 12. Logan's men were met there by a Confederate brigade under Brig. Gen John Gregg, resulting in a sharp clash that lasted several hours. Driven from the field, Gregg's outmanned infantry and artillery fell back to Jackson. Union and Confederate casualties amounted to 442 and 515 respectively. Confederate resistance at Raymond indicated to Grant that Jackson might be held more strongly than he had anticipated, and rumors reached the Union commander that strong reinforcements under Johnston were expected there. On May 13, convinced that he would have to deal with Jackson before striking at Vicksburg, Grant wheeled his entire army toward the east.

Johnston arrived by rail in Jackson on the evening of May 13 to personally supervise operations for the defense of Vicksburg. Notified that Grant's army was between Pemberton's forces and the 6,000 Confederate troops in the Jackson area, Johnston telegraphed Richmond: "I am too late."

Sherman and McPherson approached Jackson from the southwest and west, respectively, on the morning of May 14 in a pouring rain. Elements of Gregg's, William H. T. Walker's, and States Rights Gist's brigades were posted on the approaches to the city with instructions to hold just long enough for valuable supplies to be removed northward to Canton. Delaying their attack until the rain slackened to avoid spoiling their powder, the Union infantry charged the Confederate lines, drove them back, and captured the city along with 17 guns and much equipment. Having intercepted a dispatch from Johnston to Pemberton ordering the junction of all Confederate troops, Grant put two of his three corps on the road toward Edwards Station at daylight on

May 15. His plan was to drive a wedge between the Confederate forces before Johnston, circling to the north, could join up with Pemberton. Sherman remained in Jackson to destroy the railroad, supply, and manufacturing facilities.

Events preceding the battle of Champion Hill underscored the diverging strategic views of the two Confederate commanders. Pemberton opposed any move that might endanger Vicksburg. Johnston believed that Admiral Porter's passage of the batteries and Grant's approach from the rear had already doomed the city, making it valuable only for the military supplies and troops it contained. In Johnston's eyes, the South's only chance to hold the Mississippi was for Pemberton and himself to join forces and fight the great battle that would destroy Grant's army.

On the morning of May 14, Pemberton was at Bovina Station east of Vicksburg when he received the dispatch from Johnston (a copy of which Grant had already intercepted) informing him of the position of Union troops at Clinton, between the two Confederate forces, and ordering him "if practicable, [to] come up on his [Grant's] rear at once." Convinced that Johnston's recent arrival on the field and his separation from the main body did not give him sufficient information to assess the situation accurately, Pemberton called a council of war and placed the order before his commanders. Most of the council favored obeying Johnston's order, but Pemberton considered it "suicidal" and refused to endorse it on the grounds that, should anything go wrong, Vicksburg would be defenseless. He preferred to hold his troops along the line of the Big Black and confront the Federals there. Sensing that his officers were in no mood for continued inactivity, however, he agreed to lead an attack against Grant's communications, which were believed essential to the Union army's existence away from the river.

On May 15 Pemberton marched to the southeast from near Edwards Station with 23,000 men, his route further separating him from Johnston to the northeast. Meanwhile, Grant continued to push westward toward Vicksburg, continuing to exploit the wedge he had driven between Johnston's and Pemberton's forces. On the morning of the 16th Pemberton received a dispatch from Johnston ordering him to move to the northeast and unite with Johnston's force. Pemberton obeyed this order, but as his troops were countermarching they were struck near Champion Hill by forward elements of Grant's advancing army.

The battle of Champion Hill centered around a crescent-shaped ridge some 75 feet higher in elevation than the surrounding countryside near the Champion plantation home. At stake was the control of three converging roads leading from the east toward Edwards Station. Of Pemberton's three divisions, Loring's covered the Raymond Road, Bowen's was in position on Loring's left, and Carter L. Stevenson's guarded the Middle and Jackson roads. The battle opened in earnest around 10:30 a.m. on the 16th, when Brig. Gen. Alvin P. Hovey's Union division attacked along the Jackson Road, (the north road), which passed over the crest of Champion Hill. General Logan's division drove against the ridge on Hovey's right. From the crest, Stevenson's troops opened a heavy fire on the advancing Union lines, but were driven back in bitter fighting. Bowen's division, shifted north to reinforce Stevenson's battered brigades, counterattacked on Hovey's front and forced the Federals from the slopes and crest of the hill.

A Union assault during the Battle of Champion Hill. A Union officer called this battle "one of the most obstinate and murderous conflicts of the war." Newspaper correspondent Sylvanus Cadwallader of the Chicago Times, thought it "terrible" and "as hotly contested as any can be. The rattle of musketry was incessant for hours. Cannons thundered til the heavens seemed bursting. Dead men and wounded, lay strewed everywhere."

37

Grant was now compelled to reinforce his hard-pressed right. Massed Union artillery batteries opened a concentrated fire on the ridge, followed by heavy and repeated infantry attacks along the entire line. For the third time the hill changed hands. Pemberton was unable to rally his troops against these attacks, and the divisions of Bowen and Stevenson retreated. Loring's division managed to hold the Raymond Road open long enough for the rest of the army to withdraw across Baker Creek, but was cut off from the main body when Federal artillery brought the crossing under fire. (Loring was finally able to join Johnston after a long three-day march.) Pemberton retreated toward Vicksburg and that night took up positions along Big Black River about 12 miles east of Vicksburg.

The battle of Champion Hill (or Bakers Creek, as it is sometimes called) was the bloodiest action of the Vicksburg campaign. Federal troops on the field numbered 32,000; Confederates totaled 23,000. Pemberton lost nearly 4,000 men, not counting Loring's division, which never returned to his army. Grant listed casualties of 2,500, with Hovey losing one-third of his division killed and wounded.

Not knowing that Loring's division had been cut off, Pemberton intended to make a stand at the Big Black River to hold the bridges open for Loring to rejoin the main force. The Confederates had constructed a line of earthworks across the mile-wide bottomland enclosed in a loop of the river. Now, with their backs to the river, troops of Bowen's division and Brig. Gen. John C. Vaughn's reinforced brigade awaited the Union onslaught.

Before dawn on the 17th, the Union army continued its march toward Vicksburg. Grant, still hoping to win the race for the city, had sent Sherman's corps along a parallel route to the north. At mid-morning, McClernand's corps sighted the Confederate line and prepared to assault. Before the deployment was complete, Brig. Gen. Michael Lawler's brigade charged "with a shout" and smashed the Confederate center held by Vaughn's Tennesseans. Other Federal units drove against the ruptured line, causing the Confederates to break and head for the bridges in disorder. After his army's withdrawal, Pemberton ordered the bridges burned, effectively halting Union pursuit. In the confusion Grant captured more than 1,700 prisoners along with 18 artillery pieces.

As Pemberton's army fell back toward the defenses of Vicksburg, Grant's engineers began construction of bridges across the Big Black River. Trees, cotton bales, and lumber from nearby buildings were used as bridging materials. The bridges were completed by torchlight during the night. A portion of Sherman's corps crossed on the night of May 17 and were the first Union troops across the river. On the following morning, May 18, McClernand's corps crossed the river near the burned railroad bridge; McPherson's corps crossed near Amsterdam. The rest of Sherman's corps, utilizing the only pontoon bridge carried by Grant's army, crossed the river at Bridgeport.

The Union army, now within a few miles of its long-sought objective, had in 18 days completed one of the most noteworthy campaigns of the war. Marching deep into enemy territory, it had successfully, in part, lived off the country while fighting and winning five engagements and inflicting critical losses in men and equipment, had prevented Johnston and Pemberton from joining forces, and had driven the Army of Vicksburg into the defenses of the city.

As Pemberton's army fell back toward the defenses of Vicksburg, Grant's engineers began construction of bridges across the Big Black River.

By noon of May 18, with Grant's advance expected momentarily, Pemberton believed the defenses of Vicksburg were strong enough to stand off the Union army until Johnston received sufficient reinforcements to raise the expected siege and prevent the loss of the Mississippi River. There, while inspecting his defenses, Pemberton received a dispatch from Johnston advising him not to stay and try to defend the city, which Johnston felt was already doomed. Military necessity demanded, he wrote, "that instead of losing both troops and place, we must, if possible, save the troops. If it is not too late, evacuate Vicksburg and its dependencies and march to the northeast."

Unwilling to yield the city without a fight, Pemberton assembled another council of war and placed the order before his senior officers. They were of unanimous opinion that it would be "impossible to withdraw the army from this position with such morale as to be of further service to the Confederacy." As the council reached its decision to remain and fight, Union guns opened on the works. The siege of Vicksburg had begun.

Heavy guns like these were used in Federal siege batteries against the Confederate defenses.

The Siege

In September 1862 Confederate engineers had begun constructing a fortified line to protect Vicksburg against an attack from the rear. For the most part, this line of strong defense works had been thrown up along the crests of commanding ridges fronted by deep ravines. The line began at Fort Hill on the bluffs overlooking the Mississippi 1½ miles north of Vicksburg, curved for 9 miles along the ridges, and returned to the river at South Fort, 3 miles below the city. River batteries mounting heavy guns were positioned on the crest, slope, or base of the bluffs at intervals along a 4½- mile line, extending from the Water Battery in front of Fort Hill to South Fort.

Artillery positions and forts (lunettes, redans, and redoubts) had been constructed at salient and commanding points along the exterior line. The earth parapets of the forts were up to 20 feet thick. In front of most of these the Confederates had dug a deep, wide ditch so that any assaulting troops that managed to reach the work would still have a high steep wall to climb to get into it. Lines of rifle-pits or entrenchments, for the most part protected by parapets and ditches, covered the ground between the strong points. Where spurs jutted out from the main ridges, forward artillery batteries provided a deadly crossfire against attacking lines. During the early phase of the siege, the Confederates mounted as many as 115 cannon (including a few heavy siege guns) along the defense perimeter. The River Batteries contained an additional 31 heavy guns and some field pieces.

The area's topography greatly strengthened the Confederate position. Over the centuries, running water had eroded the region's soil into deep gullies and ravines, creating a broken and complicated terrain that seriously obstructed Union movements. The Confederates had cut down most of the trees fronting their lines to permit a clear field of fire and to further hinder advancing troops. Several hundred yards away, roughly parallel to the Confederate position, was a ridge system not so continuous and more broken than that occupied by Pemberton's army. Along this

41

The two men most responsible for fortifying Vicksburg were Maj. Gen. Martin Luther Smith, above, who had previously helped to plan the defenses of New Orleans, and his chief engineer, Maj. Samuel H. Lockett, below. At the time of Farragut's 1862 naval attack, Smith was Vicksburg's commanding officer. During the 1863 siege, he commanded Pemberton's left wing.

line the Union army would eventually take position and begin siege operations.

On the scattered natural bridges of high ground spanning the ravines, six roads and one railroad entered Vicksburg. To guard these access points, the Confederates had constructed nine defensive works – Fort Hill on the river north of the city, Stockade Redan, Third Louisiana Redan, Great Redoubt, Second Texas Lunette, Railroad Redoubt, Fort Garrott (also known as Square Fort), Salient Work, and South Fort on the river below Vicksburg. The Confederate divisions defending the city were, north to south, those commanded by Maj. Gen. Martin L. Smith, Maj. Gen. John H. Forney, and Maj. Gen. Stevenson. Maj. Gen. Bowen's division was held in reserve. The Army of Vicksburg at the beginning of the siege numbered about 31,000 men. Grant listed his strength, shortly after the siege began, at 50,000.

By midday of May 19 Grant had deployed 20,000 of those troops behind Vicksburg. In the north, Sherman's corps was in position opposite the Confederate left, extending from the river (at the present location of the national cemetery) to Graveyard Road. McPherson's corps, on Sherman's left, stretched from near Graveyard Road to near Baldwin's Ferry Road, while the front of McClernand's corps extended from Baldwin's Ferry Road southward toward the Square Fort. About 500 yards separated the opposing armies.

Grant had had little opportunity to assess the strength of the Vicksburg defenses because Confederate skirmishers had slowed his army's approach, thus preventing a close inspection of the Southern fortifications. Nevertheless, the Union commander decided to launch an immediate attack, reasoning that the longer he waited the stronger those defenses would become. He ordered an assault for 2 p.m. on the 19th.

Sherman's troops, whose early arrival had enabled Grant to launch the attack, advanced under heavy fire against the Confederate left. Although they got close to the works, they failed to breach the defenses and withdrew. McPherson and McClernand, not yet in good position for attack, could do little more than advance several hundred yards closer to the defense line. Grant lost 1,000 men testing the Vicksburg defenses and discovered an unyielding army manning the works. Confederate losses were slight.

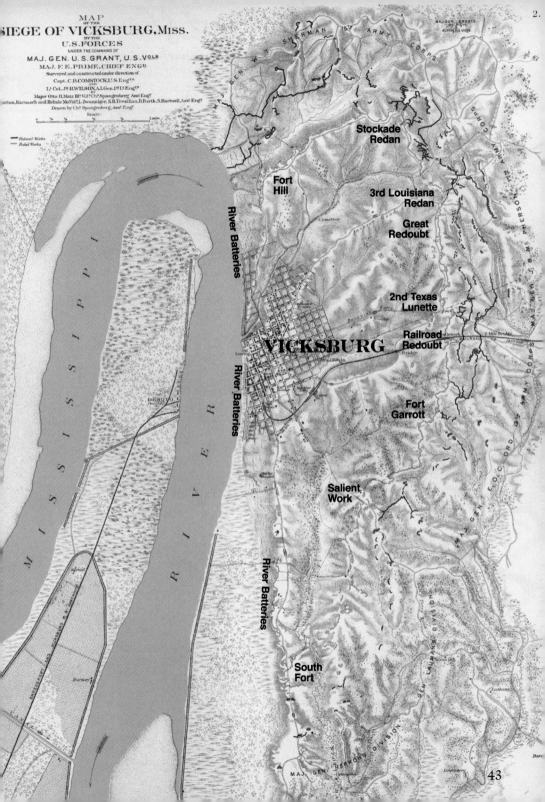

MAP
OF THE
SIEGE OF VICKSBURG, MISS.
BY THE
U.S. FORCES
UNDER THE COMMAND OF
MAJ. GEN. U.S. GRANT, U.S. VOLS
MAJ. F. E. PRIME, CHIEF ENGR

Surveyed and constructed under direction of
Capt. C.B.COMSTOCK.U.S.Engrs
and
Lt. Col. Js H.WILSON, A.I.Gen.1st Lt Engrs
by
Major Otto H.Matz IIIrd Volr Ch.f Spangenberg Assr Engf
utton,Karwasch and Helmle Mo.Volt.,L.Zwanziger, S.R.Tresillian, B.Barth, S.Hartwell,Assr Engs
Drawn by Ch.f Spangenberg, Assr Engf

Scale

Federal Works
Rebel Works

MISSISSIPPI

RIVER

River Batteries

River Batteries

River Batteries

VICKSBURG

Stockade
Redan

Fort
Hill

3rd Louisiana
Redan

Great
Redoubt

2nd Texas
Lunette

Railroad
Redoubt

Fort
Garrott

Salient
Work

South
Fort

How the Siege Was Conducted

During the siege of Vicksburg, Union troops relied extensively on approach trenches to gain protected positions close to the Confederate defense perimeter. These zigzag approaches or "saps" were deep enough to conceal troops. Thirteen major approaches, each with a network of parallels, bombproofs, and artillery emplacements, were carried forward by pick and shovel details. A Federal infantryman later recalled that, "Every man in the investing line became an army engineer day and night. The soldiers worked at digging narrow, zigzag approaches to the rebel works. Entrenchments, rifle pits, and dirt caves were made in every conceivable direction." More than 60,000 feet of trenches and 89 artillery positions, mounting 220 guns, were completed.

With an almost limitless ammunition supply, Federal artillerymen and sharpshooters (like those at Battery Hickenlooper, west of the Shirley House, in the engraving below) kept up a relentless fire, giving Confederate marksmen little opportunity to pick off the work parties which continued digging throughout the siege. Pemberton's ammunition supply dwindled daily. Faced with the possibility that no

44

more would be available, he believed it "a matter of vital importance that every charge of ammunition on hand should be hoarded with the most jealous care" and issued strict orders that both rifle-muskets and cannon should be fired only when absolutely necessary. This prevented the Confederates from keeping up the steady, harassing fire needed to check the Union's siege activities.

Only when the Union trenches approached close to the defensive works were determined efforts made to halt the Union threat. As a result of minimal Confederate artillery fire, Union artillery supremacy, and cover afforded by the approaches, Federal losses during the siege, after the assaults of May 19 and May 22, were comparatively light.

Although the probing operation of the 19th had failed, Grant did not despair but continued to ponder what important results a successful assault would achieve. Such a move, however costly, would save a long siege. In the end, fewer men might be lost and a growing threat to the Union rear – General Johnston raising troops near Jackson for the relief of Vicksburg – could be eliminated by quickly capturing Vicksburg and throwing the entire Union strength against Johnston. In addition, the Federal troops, spirited by recent victories and impatient to seize the prize for which they had campaigned so long, would work more zealously in the trenches with pick and shovel if they were certain that a siege was the only alternative. With 40,000 troops available, Grant issued orders on the 21st for another assault against Vicksburg the following day.

The Union assault of May 22 was centered against the Confederate line along a 3½-mile front from a point midway between Fort Hill and Stockade Redan to Square Fort. The felled trees and thick undergrowth, as well as the precipitous faces of the ravines, restricted the scope of Union maneuver. In preparation for the attack, field batteries were run forward and emplaced to provide a covering fire for the infantry, and troops were advanced into concealed positions – in places within 200 yards of their objective. To prevent Pemberton from shifting his forces from one threatened point to another, the infantry attacks were to begin simultaneously at 10 a.m. Watches of all Union commanders were synchronized. Reserves were posted to exploit a breakthrough.

The attack on the Stockade Redan by Maj. Gen. Francis P. Blair's division of Sherman's corps exemplified the day's action in method and result. Blair's men were faced with formidable obstacles: the route of advance along the Graveyard Road was covered by Confederate fire, and access to the redan itself was rendered difficult by steep exterior slopes and by a deep ditch fronting the works. The night before, Sherman had decided that a bridge would be needed by his men to span the ditch. Only one source of lumber could be found – a frame house in which General Grant was sleeping. Informed of the need, Grant dressed and watched the house quickly torn down for bridging material.

At the stroke of 10, the artillery bombardment of the fortifications ceased and the "Forlorn Hope," a volunteer

One of Pemberton's wing commanders during the siege was Maj. Gen. John H. Forney, who came to Vicksburg from Mobile where he headed the Department of Southern Alabama and West Florida

46

Maj. Gen. John A.
McClernand commanded the
Federal XIII Corps during
most of the Vicksburg
campaign. Vain and
extremely ambitious, his desire
for independent command
caused frequent clashes with
fellow officers, including
Grant himself. McClernand's
public criticism of the way the
campaign and siege were
being conducted eventually led
Grant to replace him.

Maryland-born Maj. Gen.
Edward O. C. Ord, a
longtime friend of Sherman's,
replaced McClernand as
commander of the XIII Corps.
Ord continued to serve Grant
as a corps and army
commander until the end of
the war.

force of 150 men, surged along Graveyard Road toward the redan. They carried planks to bridge the ditch and ladders to scale the steep exterior slope. The Confederates held their fire until the column issued from a cut in the road 400 feet away. Then the Southern soldiers "rose from their reclining position behind the works, and gave them such a terrible volley of musketry" that the road soon was nearly obstructed by the bodies of the killed and wounded, "the very sticks and chips scattered over the ground jumping under the hot shower of Rebel bullets."

A Federal color-bearer managed to place a flag on the exterior slope. The galling fire forced the remnants of attack formations that had reached the redan to take cover in the ditch. Attempting to prevent the defenders from firing down into the ditch, Federal infantry swept the top of the redan with withering volleys. The Confederates fought back, using artillery shells as hand grenades and rolling them down among the Union troops pinned in the ditch. In the face of ferocious resistance, the morning attack ground to a halt at the Stockade Redan.

Union flags were also placed on the slopes of the Railroad Redoubt, the Great Redoubt, and at the rifle-pits near the Second Texas Lunette. At the Railroad Redoubt a tenuous breach was made in the Confederate defenses by McClernand's troops. A small band of Iowans led by Sgts. Joseph Griffith and Nicholas Messenger crawled through a gap blasted by Union artillery at the salient angle, entered the redoubt, and drove out most of the remaining defenders. Later a dozen Confederates inside the redoubt surrendered. Other Federal troops clung to the slopes or took cover in the ditch.

Encouraged by his partial success, McClernand asked Grant for reinforcements and a renewal of the attacks. One of McPherson's divisions marched to augment McClernand's striking power. Grant ordered Sherman and McPherson to create a diversion in McClernand's favor. All assaults in the afternoon were shattered by a resolute Confederate defense.

48

A Federal color-bearer managed to place a flag on the exterior slope. The galling fire forced the remnants of attack formations that had reached the redan to take cover in the ditch. The Confederates fought back, using artillery shells as hand grenades and rolling them down among the Union troops pinned in the ditch. In the face of ferocious resistance, the morning attack ground to a halt at the Stockade Redan.

Responding to a call for volunteers to evict the Federals clinging to the Railroad Redoubt, picked men of Waul's Texas Legion late in the afternoon counterattacked and cleared the redoubt of enemy troops. The gap in the Confederate lines was sealed.

The afternoon attacks, the last massive assault against Vicksburg, served only to increase Federal losses and to intensify an already bitter controversy over McClernand's military performance. Union casualties on May 22 totaled 3,200. A month later McClernand was replaced by Maj. Gen. Edward O. C. Ord.

After May 25, when Grant began siege operations, only two attempts were made to break through the Confederate defenses, neither of which succeeded. Sherman, holding the Union right opposite the strong Fort Hill position, determined to neutralize the upper river batteries with naval aid. On May 27 the gunboat *Cincinnati*, protected by logs and bales of hay, moved into position and engaged the several river batteries of that sector. Subjected to a deadly plunging fire which "went entirely through our protection – hay, wood and iron," *Cincinnati* went down with her colors nailed to the stump of a mast.

*On May 27 the Union gunboat **Cincinnati** was sunk by cannon fire from the Confederate river batteries.*

A month later the Federals attempted to pierce the defense line by exploding a mine under the 3ᵈ Louisiana Redan. From the head of Logan's Approach, which had reached the exterior slope of the redan, a tunnel was dug under the three-sided fort and packed with 2,200 pounds of powder. Meanwhile, the Confederate garrison had heard the miners' picks at work beneath the redan and began a countermine in a grim race for survival. On June 25, as the entire Union line opened fire to prevent the Southerners from shifting reinforcements, the mine was detonated. The blast severely damaged the redan and gouged out a crater 40 feet wide and 12 feet deep. The 45ᵗʰ Illinois Infantry Regiment leaped from the approach and drove forward. Having anticipated this kind of maneuver, the redan's garrison had previously withdrawn to a new defense position to the rear. Now the Confederates pinned down the Illinoisans, and soldiers from other states, in the crater under a murderous fire. A sharp firefight continued for the next 26 hours, then the Federals withdrew. A second mine was detonated under the redan on July 1; still others were being prepared by Union engineers at the time of the surrender.

story continues on page 62

The Federals attempted to pierce the defense line by exploding a mine under the 3ᵈ Louisiana Redan. A tunnel was dug under the three-sided fort and packed with 2,200 pounds of gunpowder.

Explosion of the mine under the Third Louisiana Redan, June 25. The Union attack that followed, spearheaded by the 45th Illinois Infantry, was one of the most ferocious of the war.

The Federals leaped from the approach and drove forward. The redan's Confederate garrison had previously withdrawn to a new defense position to the rear. Now the Confederates pinned down the Federals in the crater under a murderous fire.

The Siege of Vicksburg, The Fight in the Cr

Gen. LOGAN's Division, G

MIDDLETON STROBRIDGE, & C.º LITH. CIN. O.

of Fort Hill, after the explosion, June 25 63.   55

PHERSON'S Army Corps.

Vicksburg Under Fire

Vicksburg, shown at right in a photograph taken during one of many periodic bombardments, lay under siege for 47 days, the only sizable American city ever to undergo such an ordeal. During much of that time it was ringed so tightly that, according to one Confederate soldier, "a cat could not have crept out... without being discovered." That the city held out as long as it did is tribute not only to the dedication and courage of its defenders but the strength of its defenses as well.

As originally laid out in September 1862, the land defenses of Vicksburg began at Fort Hill on the bluffs above the city and, after following an irregular course of hills and ridges, ended at South Fort, 3 miles below the city.

When the siege began, the Union army had no heavy artillery. As a result, General Grant had to rely initially on field batteries like this one from the Wisconsin Light Artillery, photographed outside Vicksburg, to bombard the Confederate defenses. On June 5 the Federals began to emplace heavy artillery from Admiral Porter's gunboats on the siege lines. They continued to add new pieces right up to the day of the surrender.

The Napoleon 12-pounder, Model 1857 cannon, shown here, was a common smoothbore artillery piece used by both sides during the war. Originally developed in France in the 1850s, it could fire shot, shell, spherical case, and canister, and had an effective range of just under a mile. Both Union and Confederate artillerymen admired it for its accuracy and safety record.

Overlooking the Mississippi the Confederates established heavy artillery positions called "River Batteries" at intervals along the bluff line from Fort Hill to South Fort. These pieces were employed either on the crest, slope, or base of the bluffs.

One of Grant's officers, clearly impressed with what he saw, described the Confederate works as "A long line of high, rugged, irregular bluffs, clearly cut against the sky, crowned with cannon which peered ominously from embrasures to the right

and left as far as the eye could see...The approaches to this position were frightful." Still, as Grant's lines tightened and grew ever closer, perceptive soldiers could see that there could be only one final outcome.

The 32-pounder smoothbore seacoast cannon, shown in the drawing at left, was one of the mainstays of Vicksburg's river defenses. Like the 12-pounder Napoleon, it fired shot, shell case, and canister. It could also fire grapeshot and had a slightly greater range.

A siege battery of Hovey's division, McClernand's Corps, fires on a part of the Confederate line held by General Stevenson.

Life in the Trenches

Siege life for the Confederate soldiers was a hazardous ordeal; nearly 3,200 were killed or wounded. Pemberton's limited number of troops forced him to keep almost his entire army in the trenches fulltime, enduring sun, rain, mud, poor and inadequate food, as well as the bullets and shells of the Union army for 47 days and nights.

Rations were generally prepared by details of soldiers behind the lines and carried to the troops at the breastworks. Coffee, the soldier's staple, was soon unobtainable and an ersatz beverage introduced, the somewhat questionable ingredients of which included sweet potatoes, blackberry leaves, and sassafras. To replace the exhausted flour

supply, a substitute was devised from ground peas and cornmeal – "a nauseous composition," according to one soldier, with "the properties of India-rubber" and "worse than leather to digest." A more famous, although not necessarily a more palatable, item of the besieged soldiers' diet was the mule meat introduced late in the siege.

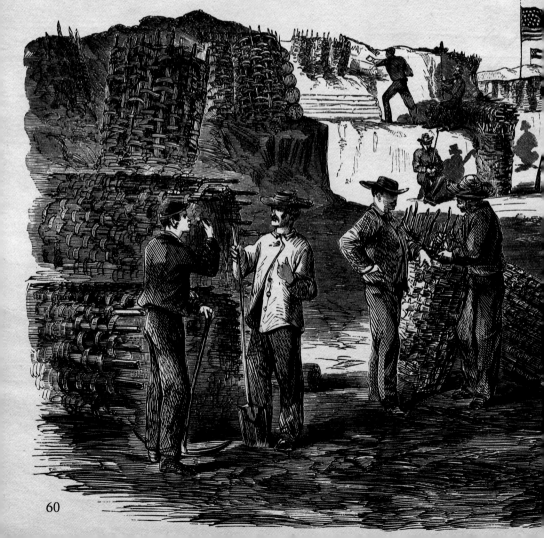

For protection against Union artillery fire, the Confederate troops dug bomb-proofs in the reverse slope of their fortified ridge (much like those dug by their Federal counterparts around the Shirley House in the photograph on page 63). From these dugouts, bulwarked by heavy timbers, trenches connected with the fortifications, affording the besieged some degree of relaxation in reading or playing cards a few yards from the front line.

Trench life for Grant's men was much the same but not so rigorous or dangerous. Food supplies were ample, although lack of pure water was a problem for both armies and brought on considerable sickness. When not on the siege line or relaxing, Federal soldiers were kept busy making such things as gabions, the cylindrical-shaped baskets shown in the engraving below which, when filled with earth, helped to protect approach trenches and artillery positions.

By the beginning of July the Army of Vicksburg had held the line for six weeks, but its unyielding defense had been a costly one. Pemberton reported 10,000 of his men so debilitated by wounds and sickness as to be no longer able to man the works, and the list of ineffectives swelled daily from the twin afflictions of insufficient rations and the devastating fire of Union artillery and the searching volleys of Union sharpshooters. Each day the constricting Union line pushed closer against the Vicksburg defenses, and there were indications that Grant might soon launch another great assault which, even if repulsed, must certainly result in a severe toll of the garrison.

Pemberton's foremost objective in prolonging the defense of Vicksburg was to afford Johnston and the Confederate government time to collect sufficient troops to raise the siege. Unfortunately, circumstances worked against his plan. Gen. Robert E. Lee's Army of Northern Virginia began its invasion of the North shortly after Grant invested the city, and no troops could be spared from that quarter. Only a limited number of men were available from other areas.

By the first week of June, reinforcements from Tennessee, South Carolina, and Georgia had increased Johnston's force to 31,000 troops. Grant, anticipating that Johnston would move against his rear, was sent reinforcements from Kentucky, West Tennessee, and Missouri to construct and man a strong outer defense position facing the probable line of advance. This gave Grant two lines of works – one to hold Pemberton in, the other to keep Johnston out. While Confederate Secretary of War James A. Seddon counseled Johnston that "the eyes and hopes of the whole Confederacy are upon you, with the full confidence that you will act, and with the sentiment that it is better to fail nobly daring, than, through prudence even, to be inactive," Johnston notified his government on June 15: "I consider saving Vicksburg hopeless."

On July 1 Johnston began moving his army of four infantry divisions and one cavalry division from Jackson. He arrived July 3 at the east bank of the Big Black River, seeking a vulnerable place to attack Grant's outer defenses. His reconnaissance convinced him that no practical crossing of the Big Black River lay north of the railroad bridge. On July 5 Johnston received definite word of the fall of Vicksburg. On the following day he began withdrawing his army toward Jackson.

Brigade commander Stephen D. Lee disagreed with the decision to surrender Vicksburg but, unlike other officers, never blamed Pemberton for the defeat. Lee was later influential in the creation of Vicksburg National Military Park and served briefly as chairman of the park commission.

Efforts by Confederate forces in the Trans-Mississippi to assist the Vicksburg garrison were checked by Union troops holding the Young's Point, Milliken's Bend, and Lake Providence enclaves, supported by Admiral Porter's gunboats. At Milliken's Bend, on June 7, there was a savage fight in which a brigade of blacks suffered heavy losses during an attack by a brigade of Texans. The timely arrival of Union gunboats compelled the Texans to withdraw. This was the second Civil War battle in which blacks played a major role.

Faced with dwindling stores and no help from the outside, Pemberton saw only two eventualities: "either to evacuate the city and cut my way out or to capitulate upon the best obtainable terms." Contemplating the former possibility, he asked his division commanders on July 1 to report whether the physical condition of the troops would favor such a hazardous stroke. All but two of his division and brigade commanders were unanimous in their replies that siege conditions had physically distressed so large a number of the defending army that an attempt to cut through the Union lines would be disastrous. Pemberton's only alternative, then, was surrender.

Although not requested, Pemberton also received the verdict of his army in a message from an unknown soldier, signed "Many Soldiers." Taking pride in the gallant conduct of his fellow soldiers "in repulsing the enemy at every assault, and bearing with patient endurance all the privations and hardships," the writer requested the commanding general to "think of one small biscuit and one or two mouthfuls of bacon per day," concluding with the irrefutable logic of an enlisted man: "If you can't feed us, you had better surrender us, horrible as the idea is."

Civilian Life in Vicksburg During the Siege

For the civilian population of Vicksburg, the siege was a grim and harrowing experience. Faced with the choice of either leaving the city or sharing the fate of the army, many of the townspeople preferred to remain. They were joined by refugees accompanying the Confederate retreat into the city.

Vicksburg had been subjected to periodic naval bombardment during the preceding year and to a steady barrage during the siege. To the civilians, as to the Confederate soldiers, there seemed only three intervals during the day

when the shelling ceased – 8 a.m., noon, and 8 p.m. – when the Union artillerymen ate their meals. Much of the accustomed social life of the town continued. Men and women passed along the streets despite frequent shell explosions, and one of the town's newspapers continued to appear – finally printed on wallpaper.

Despite the artillery fire, few civilians were killed, although many dwellings were destroyed or badly damaged. "Very few houses are without evidence of the bombardment," wrote Mrs. James M. Loughborough, who had come to Vicksburg to share her soldier-husband's fate, "and yet the inhabitants live in their homes happy and contented, not knowing what moment the houses may be rent over their heads by the explosion of a shell." For relief and protection against shellfire, many of the townspeople occupied caves dug into the hillsides, like those shown in the engraving below. The caves, about the size of a large room, were sometimes provided with bed, table, chairs, and other furnishings (far left) to create what one dweller felt was a "large and habitable abode."

As the siege progressed, yellow hospital flags floated over more and more buildings. Thousands of Confederate sick and wounded were brought into the city, many being cared for by the women of Vicksburg. In the latter stages of the siege the food stores of the city were badly depleted, placing the people of Vicksburg on extremely short rations.

At 8 a.m. on July 3 Chaplain Richard L. Howard of the 124th Illinois Infantry located near the Shirley House noticed "a white flag away to our left on the rebel works. Soon another appeared, and another and, directly, one in front of us. The firing ceased, and all was still, the first time since May 25th, thirty-nine days. Soon greybacks began to show themselves all along the lines. Heads first, cautiously, then bodies, and we straightened up too, in many places only a few yards from them. The works were mounted and we looked each other in the face, the line of motley and the line of blue. How eager we all were to see, and what did it all mean?" A few hours later Grant and Pemberton met beneath an oak tree on a slope between the lines to begin negotiations for the surrender of the 29,500-man garrison. No accord was forthcoming at this meeting. Following an exchange of communications, an agreement was reached early the next morning. It had been 14 months since Farragut's warships had first engaged the Vicksburg batteries, seven months since Grant's first expedition against the city, and 47 days since the appearance of the Federal army on the city's eastern approaches. On the morning of July 4, 1863, while Northern cities celebrated Independence Day, the Army of Vicksburg was formally surrendered. The Confederate troops marched out from their defenses and stacked their rifles, cartridge-boxes, and flags before a generally hushed Union army which witnessed the historic event with little cheering – a testimonial of respect for the courageous defenders of Vicksburg, whose line was never broken.

Into the city which had defied him for so long, and which nearly proved the graveyard rather than the springboard of his military career, rode General Grant. At the courthouse, where the Stars and Bars had floated in sight of the Union army and navy throughout the siege, he watched the national colors raised on the flagstaff, and then proceeded to the waterfront. With every vessel of the navy sounding its whistle in celebration, he went aboard Porter's flagship to express his gratitude for the work of the fleet.

The surrender of Vicksburg and the simultaneous repulse of Lee's northern invasion at the Battle of Gettysburg marked the beginning of the end for the Southern Confederacy. Previously there had been confidence that victory, although demanding desperate

Maj. Gen. James Birdseye McPherson, XVII Corps commander, won the praises of both Grant and Sherman during the Vicksburg campaign. He was appointed commander of the Vicksburg district after Federal troops occupied the city on July 4.

For forty-seven days, Union shot and shell rained down on Vicksburg. Two women and a Confederate soldier shrink in terror at an unexploded Federal shell that landed near their cave dug into the hillside.

"The Shell" by Howard Pyle

At 8 a.m. on July 3 Chaplain R.L. Howard of the 124th Illinois Infantry located near the Shirley House noticed "a white flag away to our left on the rebel works. Soon another appeared, and another and, directly, one in front of us. The firing ceased, and all was still, the first time since May 25th, thirty-nine days.

measures, could yet be achieved. Now there was only the hope that the North might sicken at the frightful cost of continuing the war and terminate hostilities. The great objective of the war in the West – the opening of the Mississippi River and the severing of the Confederacy – had been realized with the fall of Vicksburg. While in the East the Union armies battled on in bloody stalemate before Richmond, the armies of the West would now launch their columns deep into the Confederacy's vitals.

Grant emerged from the Vicksburg Campaign with a hard-won reputation as a master strategist. His clear-cut victories at Vicksburg and subsequently at Chattanooga prompted President Lincoln, in March 1864, to place him in command of all the armies of the United States. From this position he was destined to direct the final campaigns of the war and to receive Lee's surrender at Appomattox. As for Pemberton, the fall of Vicksburg subjected him to painful criticism from those who held that a more resourceful defense might have saved the city, or his army, or both. Grant had disobeyed orders in striking behind Vicksburg alone rather than waiting to combine forces with Banks; Pemberton, on orders from Jefferson Davis, had decided to protect Vicksburg at all cost rather than joining Johnston and risk losing of the city. But Grant's gamble had succeeded and Pemberton's had failed; and in war, as a leading Confederate commander had soberly remarked, the people measure a general's merit by his successes. "I thought and still think you did right to risk an army for the purpose of keeping command of

Grant and Pemberton met beneath an oak tree on a slope between the lines to begin negotiations for the surrender of the 29,500-man garrison. No accord was forthcoming at this meeting. Following an exchange of communications, an agreement was reached early the next morning.

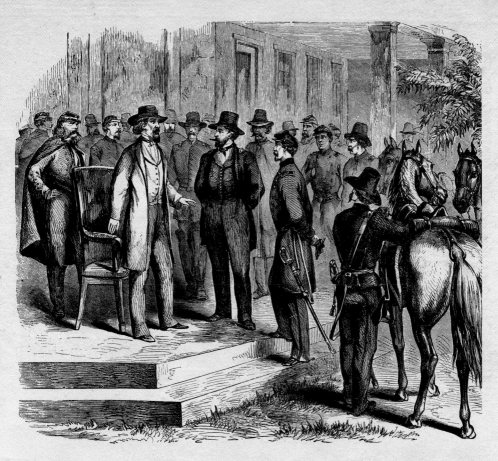

Grant was on his way to the courthouse when he saw Pemberton at the Rock House and stopped to chat.

even a section of the Mississippi River," President Davis wrote to Pemberton after the surrender. "Had you succeeded none would have blamed, had you not made the attempt few if any would have defended your course."

In the Confederate capital, Col. Josiah Gorgas, one of the most able of Southern leaders, confided to his diary the implications of the calamitous change in fortune to the South attending the twin disasters of Gettysburg and Vicksburg: "Events have succeeded one another with disastrous rapidity. One brief month ago we were apparently at the point of success. Lee was in Pennsylvania threatening Harrisburgh, and even Philadelphia. Vicksburg seemed to laugh all Grant's efforts to scorn…All looked bright. Now the picture is just as somber as it was bright then. Lee failed at Gettysburg…Vicksburg and Port Hudson capitulated, surrendering thirty-five thousand men and forty-five thousand arms. It seems incredible that human power could effect such a change in so brief a space. Yesterday we rode on the pinnacle of success – today absolute ruin seems to be our portion. The Confederacy totters to its destruction."

In Washington, a grateful President Lincoln sat at his desk seeking words to express appreciation to Grant "for the almost inestimable service" he had done the country. Explaining the fear he had entertained that the Union army might be destroyed during its daring thrust in the rear of Vicksburg, which he believed at the time to be a "mistake," Lincoln wrote to Grant: "I wish now to make the personal acknowledgement that you were right and I was wrong."

On July 9 the Confederate commander at Port Hudson, upon learning of the fall of Vicksburg, surrendered his garrison of 6,000 men. One week later the merchant steamboat *Imperial* tied up at the wharf at New Orleans, completing the 1,200-mile passage from St. Louis undisturbed by hostile guns. After two years of land and naval warfare, the grip of the South had been broken – the Mississippi River was open, and merchant and military traffic now enjoyed unrestricted passage to its mouth. In the words of Lincoln, "The Father of Waters again goes unvexed to the sea."

The victorious General Grant and the Federal army enters Vicksburg. July 4, 1863. At the courthouse, where the Stars and Bars had floated in sight of the Union army and navy throughout the siege, he watched the national colors raised on the flagstaff, and then proceeded to the waterfront.

*Arrival of the **Imperial** in New Orleans after the opening of the Mississippi River*

USS *Cairo*: Vicksburg's Naval Legacy

When Adm. David D. Porter took over the Mississippi Squadron from Flag Officer Charles H. Davis in October 1862, his total command consisted of some 125 vessels of all kinds. The ironclad river gunboats, however, most of which had been built by James B. Eads over the course of a few short months, were the backbone of the squadron. The gunboats had already compiled a distinguished record, first under Flag Officer Andrew H. Foote and then under Davis. Under Porter they would continue to distinguish themselves on the vast stretches of the Mississippi and its tributaries, most notably in Maj. Gen. Ulysses S. Grant's 1862-63 operations against Vicksburg.

Over the course of Grant's long Vicksburg campaign, during which naval cooperation was critical, many of Porter's ironclad gunboats were damaged and some were sunk. One of the first casualties was the USS *Cairo*, shown below in a wartime photograph. On December 12, 1862, preparatory to Maj. Gen. William T. Sherman's advance to Chickasaw Bayou, *Cairo*, commanded by Lt. Cmdr. Thomas O. Selfridge (left) and accompanied by several other boats, steamed up the Yazoo River, north of Vicksburg, to protect light-draft

vessels clearing Confederate mines from the channel.

Suddenly, two explosions in quick succession tore gaping holes in the boat's bottom. Within minutes the ironclad lay on the bottom of the river, only the tops of her chimneys and flagstaffs above the water. *Cairo* had become the first vessel in history to be sunk by an electrically detonated mine.

It is not for this, however, or her generally unspectacular war record that *Cairo* has won a lasting place in history; rather it is for what went down with her when she sank in the Yazoo. Here was preserved, in time-capsule form, information about naval construction, naval stores, armament, and the personal gear of the crew who served on board.

The vast array of artifacts recovered from the gunboat before and after it was salvaged in the early 1960s is now on display at the USS Cairo Museum adjacent to Vicksburg National Cemetery. These, together with the remains of the gunboat herself, give new insight into naval life during the Civil War years.

Raised from her watery grave, **Cairo** was brought to the park in 1977 and now rests on a concrete foundation outside the Museum entrance. The boat has been partially restored.

USS *Cairo* Museum

The USS *Cairo* Museum is located adjacent to the Vicksburg National Cemetery and can be reached from the park tour road or through the city via Cherry Street, Fort Hill Road, and Connecting Avenue. It is open daily, except Thanksgiving, Christmas and New Year's Day.

Here within a symbolic triangular-shaped building denoting war and aggression is displayed a significant cross section of artifacts recovered from the ironclad river gunboat *Cairo*, which went down in the Yazoo River on December 12, 1862, the first vessel in naval history to be sunk by an electrically detonated mine.

When *Cairo* sank, her crew managed to save only what they were carrying. When she was raised in 1964, her storerooms yielded a wealth of artifacts, including many of the sailors' personal possessions put there for safekeeping. Many of these relics are displayed in the museum and provide a real insight into naval life during the Civil War.

Artifacts in the museum include weaponry, tableware, ship's rigging and hardware, lighting devices, tools and fasteners, medical supplies and bottles, uniform parts and accessories, and personal belongings. Each grouping of artifacts tells part of the story.

Cairo's armament consisted of three 8-inch Navy smoothbore cannon, one 30-pounder Parrott rifle, six 32-pounder Navy smoothbores, and three rifled Army 42-pounders. All were recovered between September 20, 1960, and November 6, 1963, and all but one, the 32-pounder smoothbore shown being hoisted from the water in the photograph at right, were found to be loaded. The guns are now mounted aboard *Cairo* exhibited outside the museum.

The USS *Cairo* is the sole survivor of the Mississippi Squadron. This boat is a monument to the vessels and crews on both sides that fought for the river that controlled America's future. In naval terms, they were "able to navigate heavy dew." The infantry nicknamed them "turtlebacks" or "turtles." To the inland navy, they were things of beauty. Admiral Foote complained their six-knot speed "almost too slow," but Captain William Porter of the *Essex* interjected, "Plenty fast enough to fight with."

's bow and stern section at Pascagoula, Mississippi, after the boat was raised from the Yazoo River in 1962.

The type of torpedo that sank the U.S.S. Cairo. From a sketch in the Official Records of the Union and Confederate Navies.

U.S.S Cairo
Commissioned: January 15, 1862
Sunk: December 12, 1862
Site of Sinking: 16 miles from the mouth of Yazoo River
Cause: Torpedo (mine)
Depth at Site: 6 fathoms (36 feet)

Sketch of the boat's wreck, entitled "Cairo Submerged", probably depicting the scene immediately after she was sunk by a Confederate mine in the Yazoo River, Mississippi, on December 12, 1862. Note men sitting on projecting timbers and swimming in the water nearby.

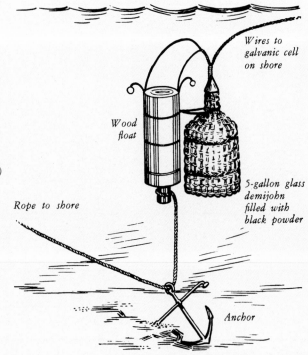

Wires to galvanic cell on shore

Wood float

5-gallon glass demijohn filled with black powder

Rope to shore

Anchor

Some of the crews' personal objects recovered from the sunken gunboat are shown here. Thanks to the mud that nearly encases the boat, most were remarkably well preserved despite being underwater for more than a century.

VICKSBURG CAMPAIGN

Thickness of Plate Armor: 2-1/2 inches
Total Weight of Armor: 122 tons
Armor Plate Size: 13 inches wide by 8-1/2 feet to 11 feet long
Material: Charcoal iron
Location: Casemate front and casemate sides to protect boilers
Rail Armor: Added after the Battle of Memphis on forward side casemates
Ranges of Wood: 19-1/2 inches to 26 inches

Length: 175'0"   Officers: 17
Width: 51'2"   Petty Officers: 27
Draft: 6'0"   Seamen: 111
Tonnage: 512 tons   Landsmen: 3
Full Load: 888 tons   Apprentices: 1
Speed: 6 knots   Firemen: 12
                             Coal Heavers: 4
                             TOTAL Crew: 175

Vicksburg Battlefield Today

Cannon barrels are authentic Civil War types; most of the iron carriages were replaced in the last five years. Cannon are located on sites occupied by artillery pieces during the siege. Excluding ravines, only scattered trees dotted the battlefield in 1863. Today's dense growth stems from trees planted in the 1930s.

Things to See and Do

structures commemorating the heroism and sacrifices of their fighting men. Statues honor military and civilian figures. Bronze busts and relief portraits identify brigade and division commanders.

Cannon barrels are authentic Civil War types; most of the iron carriages were replaced in the last five years. Cannon are located on sites occupied by artillery pieces during the siege. Excluding ravines, only scattered trees dotted the battlefield in 1863. Today's dense growth stems from trees planted in the 1930s.

Vicksburg National Military Park was established in 1899 to preserve the site of the siege of Vicksburg, and was placed under the jurisdiction of the War Department. In August 1933 it was transferred to the National Park Service. Most significant areas of the Union siege line and the Confederate defense perimeter lie within park boundaries. Sixteen miles of roads provide access to nearly 2,000 acres of park land, and national cemetery, featuring restored forts, rifle-pits, and battery positions, 150 artillery pieces, and more than 1,350 monuments, markers, tablets, busts, relief portraits, and State memorials.

The park curves in a semicircle east of the Vicksburg business district. Two main roads provide access to all principal points in the park: Union Avenue, paralleling the Federal siege line, and Confederate Avenue, paralleling the Confederate defense perimeter.

Iron tablets locate vital combat areas, identify positions held by individual units, and mark reconstructed earthworks, forts, and artillery positions. Monuments erected by states include granite regimental markers and impressive granite and marble

Park Headquarters and Visitor Center are located off Clay Street (US 80, Historic) near Exit 4B, I-20. Exhibits illustrate aspects of the campaign and siege. An 20-minute film dramatizes the decisive phase of operations leading to the surrender of Vicksburg. Information and literature are available. A 16-mile self-guiding tour begins at the Memorial Arch (which commemorates the 1917 reunion of veterans who fought at Vicksburg) and follows a clearly marked route which is adapted for one-way traffic most of the distance. The following points of interest are presented in the order in which you will encounter them on your tour of the battlefield and are keyed to the map inside the back cover of this booklet.

Minnesota Memorial
At the base of the 90-foot obelisk, a symbolic figure of Peace holds a shield and a sword signifying that soldiers of both armies have placed their weapons in her keeping, and the Union is at peace.

Shirley House

Union soldiers called it "the white house," and it is the only surviving wartime structure in the park. This siege landmark served as headquarters for the 45th Illinois Infantry, members of which built numerous bombproof shelters on the slope east of the house to protect themselves against Confederate artillery. The exterior has been restored to its 1863 appearance. The interior will soon be restored and open to the public.

Michigan Memorial

A symbolic figure of the Spirit of Michigan offers laurels to her soldiers who fought in the campaign.

Battery De Golyer

From this position guns of the 8th Michigan Light Artillery Battery commanded by Captain Samuel De Golyer hammered the Confederates' Great Redoubt 700 yards to the west. At one time as many as 22 Federal artillery pieces representing several batteries were mounted here. Captain De Golyer was mortally wounded 600 yards to the north of here while directing the fire of some of his guns.

Illinois Memorial

The dome of this memorial temple is modeled after the Pantheon in Rome. The largest monument on the field, it is dedicated to the 36,325 Illinois soldiers whose names are inscribed on bronze plaques. No device indicative of war appears on the Memorial, as specified by the Illinois Commission that authorized its placement.

Third Louisiana Redan

Here was one of the major Confederate fortifications guarding the Jackson Road approach to Vicksburg. Union troops gained access to the fort by "Logan's Approach," a zigzag siege trench. Federal engineers mined the redan and on June 25 exploded 2,200 pounds of powder under it, blasting a tremendous crater into which infantry raced, only to be withdrawn after severe fighting. Another mine was detonated a week later. Neither succeeded in breaking the Confederate line.

Ransom's Gun Path

From this area cannoneers of Company F, 2ᵈ Illinois Artillery Regiment, dismantled and, with the assistance of infantrymen from Brig. Gen. Thomas E. G. Ransom's brigade, dragged two 12-pounder cannon over rugged terrain and across a bayou to a position within 100 yards of the Confederate line. There the guns were reassembled and placed in action.

Wisconsin Memorial

"Old Abe," the famous Wisconsin war eagle and mascot of Company C, 8th Wisconsin Infantry Regiment, was carried alongside the regimental colors on the march and in battle through three years of war. A six-foot high bronze replica of Old Abe standing atop the state monument honors his war service. Names of all Wisconsin soldiers at Vicksburg are recorded on plaques at the base of the shaft.

West Virginia Memorial

A heroic bust of Maj. Arza M. Goodspeed, who lost his life in the Federal assault of May 19, overlooks the position manned by the 4th West Virginia Infantry Regiment during the siege.

Stockade Redan Attack

From this and nearby points on May 19, Gen. William T. Sherman launched an infantry attack against the Stockade Redan. The Federals were repulsed with heavy losses. Three days later, as part of a general assault on the Confederate lines, Union soldiers attacked the redan again. This attack also failed.

Kansas Memorial

The bottom circle represents the prewar unity of the United States. The broken circle in the center symbolizes the Union divided by the Civil War. The perfect circle at the top depicts national unity restored by the war.

Grant's Headquarters Area

An imposing equestrian statue of General Grant marks the site of his headquarters. Nearby are impressive memorials of five northeastern States – Pennsylvania, New Hampshire, Massachusetts, New York, and Rhode Island. Troops from these states were stationed on the Federal exterior line 10 to 15 miles north and east of Vicksburg.

Thayer's Approach

Union troops of Gen. John Thayer's brigade dug an approach trench up the 200-foot high ridge close to the tree line on your right. Just before the end of the siege, the approach reached a Confederate redoubt atop the ridge. Thayer's infantrymen used the tunnel underneath the road to avoid enemy fire directed against the ridge adjoining the tour route.

U.S. Navy Memorial

The 202-foot obelisk is a tribute to the achievements of the Union Navy in the campaign to reopen the Mississippi River. Statues of four fleet commanders

Vicksburg National Cemetery was established in 1866 to reinter the remains of soldiers given temporary burial in scattered locations during the war. Thousands more died from 1866 - 1869 bringing the number of burials to 17,000 Civil War veterans. The identity of almost 13,000 soldiers and sailors is unknown.

(Admirals Farragut and Porter and Flag Officers Davis and Foote) surround the base. Between the road and the memorial, note the large bronze plaque recounting the achievements of the inland navy.

Battery Selfridge
The heavy cannon which were removed from a gunboat and mounted on this towering ridge were the only land-based artillery pieces served by naval gunners during the siege.

Vicksburg National Cemetery
Established in 1866, thousands of bodies were disintered and reburied in Vicksburg. Thousands more died during occupation between 1866 - 1869 bringing the number of burials to 17,000 Civil War veterans. The identity of almost 13,000 soldiers and sailors is unknown. The national cemetery also contains the remains of veterans of the Mexican and Spanish-American Wars, World Wars I and II, and the Korean Conflict.

USS *Cairo* Museum
Here within a symbolic triangular-shaped building denoting war and aggression is displayed a significant cross section of artifacts recovered from the ironclad river gunboat *Cairo*, which went down in the Yazoo River on December 12, 1862, the first vessel in naval history to be sunk by an electrically detonated mine.

Fort Hill
During the centuries-old struggle for control of the Mississippi, the flags of Great Britain, France, Spain, the United States, and the Confederacy have flown over this historic site where the bluffs meet the river. The waterway below the bluffs is not the Mississippi River - it changed its course in 1876 – but the Yazoo River

Diversion Canal, which brings the Yazoo River into the old bed of the Mississippi at this point. Fort Hill, the northern anchor of the Confederate defense line, was one of the strongest works protecting Vicksburg. No Federal attack was ever made against it.

Stockade Redan

From the ridge 150 yards away, Union cannon were trained on this work and blasted the Confederate defenders relentlessly. During the May 22 assault, Grant's infantry reached the fort's parapet. Two color-bearers planted their flags on the exterior slope before the attacks were broken and the assailants driven back.

Missouri Memorial

A border state, Missouri was divided in sympathy during the Civil War. Her soldiers enlisted in both Union and Confederate armies. In this sector Missouri soldiers on both sides faced and fought each other. The memorial is dedicated to both. The bronze plaque on the left depicts Missouri Federals attacking this position; the one on the right shows Missouri Confederates defending it. Between the panels a Roman galley symbolizes the ship of state; above, the Spirit of the Republic emerges from the war with new strength.

Arkansas Memorial

The twin pylons represent North and South, split by the sword of war and reunited by the cross of faith in a restored Union. Depicted on the left are Arkansas soldiers repelling a Federal assault; on the right, the Confederate ram *Arkansas*.

Surrender Interview Site

Grant and Pemberton met under an oak tree here, midway between the lines, on July 3 to begin the first phase of surrender negotiations. No agreement, however, was reached. By dawn the next day an exchange of messages had resulted in the adoption of a mutually acceptable formula for the surrender of the Army of Vicksburg. The oak tree quickly vanished to provide souvenirs of this historic event.

Note: To reach this site you will have to leave the tour route temporarily. Turn onto the first paved road to the left after crossing the bridge and proceeding up the steep hill. Drive 200 feet to the upright cannon (on your right) identifying the surrender interview site. To return to the tour route, use the loop driveway a short distance ahead on the left and reverse direction. When you reach Confederate Avenue (which is one-way) turn left.

The Great Redoubt

This, one of the largest forts on the Confederate line, guarded the Jackson Road. The Federal attack here on May 22 was repulsed with heavy Union losses. The low granite markers on the slope below the tour road mark the farthest advance that day of Illinois regiments in this sector of the battlefield. On the right side of the road, markers show the point reached by the 7th Missouri (Union) Infantry Regiment.

92

Louisiana Memorial

Erected in 1920, this 85-foot high Corinthian column surmounted by a flaming brazier, stands within the Great Redoubt, the highest natural elevation in the park. Louisiana infantry defended this area during the siege.

Mississippi Memorial

This imposing memorial honors the Mississippi soldiers who participated in the defense. The bas-relief and sculptures around the base of the shaft depict battle scenes. The 9-inch Dahlgren cannon at the rear of the monument is representative of the heavy artillery pieces employed at Vicksburg.

Pemberton Circle

Lt. Gen. John C. Pemberton, a native Pennsylvanian, elected to fight for the South and led the Army of Vicksburg. When a command in keeping with his rank of three-star general was unavailable after Vicksburg's surrender, he voluntarily resigned his commission and served as a lieutenant colonel of artillery for the remainder of the war – a testimonial of his loyalty to the South.

Second Texas Lunette

This Confederate fort, guarding the Baldwin's Ferry Road leading into Vicksburg, was manned by the 2^d Texas Infantry Regiment. It stood on the highest part of the private cemetery 500 feet to the east. Fierce fighting raged here on May 22 when the Federal offensive nearly succeeded in capturing the lunette.

Jefferson Davis Statue

Davis was a West Point graduate, Mexican War colonel, Mississippi cotton planter, United States Senator, Secretary of War, and finally, President of the Confederacy. (At this point notice the natural strength of the Confederate position on the crest of the ridge. The ground drops away on the other side of the tour route and, several hundred yards across the ravine, rises to a similar and parallel ridge. From this the Union army launched it siege operations against the Confederate line. Before the siege began, all the trees between the lines had been cut down by the Confederate engineers to insure a clear field of fire.)

Railroad Redoubt

This powerful Confederate earthwork barred access to Vicksburg by way of the Southern Railroad of Mississippi. In furious action on the morning of May 22, Federal infantry gained a tenuous foothold inside the redoubt but failed to achieve a breakthrough. In the afternoon, a detachment of Waul's Texas Legion dislodged the Union troops from the fort and sealed this breach in the Confederate lines.

Texas Memorial

Dedicated in 1961, this impressive structure of red Texas granite commemorates the valor and devotion of Texas troops who served on both sides of the Mississippi River in the Vicksburg Campaign.

Alabama Memorial

Around the flag are seven heroic men from Alabama being inspired by a woman representing the state itself. It symbolizes the courage and devotion of both the soldiers and women of Alabama during the war. The monument was dedicated in 1951.

Fort Garrott

The zigzag indentations in front of the parking area represent a partial reconstruction of Union Gen. Alvin P. Hovey's approach trenches. You can see the left and right approaches joining to form a single trench which terminates 30 yards short of Fort Garrott (also known as Square Fort.) Col. Isham W. Garrott, commanding Confederate troops in this immediate area, was killed inside the fort by a Federal sharpshooter who fired from a tree. That same day a communication was en route to Vicksburg announcing Colonel Garrott's promotion to the rank of brigadier general.

Georgia Memorial

Two hundred feet to the right of Fort Garrott a granite shaft honors Georgians who gave their lives in the Vicksburg Campaign.

Indiana Memorial

Dedicated in 1926, a heroic statue of Indiana's Civil War governor, Oliver P. Morton, towers over the tour route in a combat sector which was manned by Indiana infantry.

Hovey' Approach

This point affords a view of Fort Garrott from the Federal side of the battlefield. The course of Hovey's Right Approach is indicated by iron tablets wandering up the hillside.

Iowa Memorial

In front, a mounted color-bearer with unfurled flag awaits the order to advance. The six bronze bas-relief panels portray scenes of the Vicksburg Campaign in which Iowa soldiers participated – the bombardments of Grand Gulf, the battles of Port Gibson, Jackson, Champion Hill, and Big Black River, and the May 22 assault on Vicksburg.

Maryland Monument

Placed in 1914, this commemorative tablet honors the men of the 3d Maryland Battery commanded by Captain Ferdinand O. Claiborne, who was killed during the defense of Vicksburg. This was the only Maryland unit on either side of the battlelines at Vicksburg.

Battlefield Tour Outside the National Military Park

If you wish to tour the southerly portion of the battlefield now under municipal jurisdiction, turn right onto Clay Street (US 80 Historic), and proceed one mile west. Turn left onto Mission 66 Road and drive another mile. At this point the name of the road on which you are traveling changes to Confederate Avenue; granite monuments and iron tablets will be seen off the roadway.

The North Carolina Memorial stands off the right side of Confederate Avenue 500 feet beyond the red brick vehicular overpass, which you will cross. A granite tablet donated by the United Daughters of the Confederacy to honor Florida fighting men stands to your right, within a triangular plot in the Mulvihill Avenue intersection. Another granite tablet erected by the United Daughters of the Confederacy to commemorate South Carolina veterans is mounted on the lawn of a Vicksburg public school, to the right of the highway.

When Confederate Avenue meets a crossroad near the Parkside Theater, it turns 90 degrees to the right. On the left, just beyond this turn, a bronze plaque mounted on a granite block memorializes the Botetourt (Virginia) Artillery, the only unit in the siege from the Old Dominion. Continue past the theater to Washington Street, where three detached segments of the park are located on the bluffs overlooking the Mississippi River. Turn right and proceed several hundred feet to Louisiana Circle, which commemorates the Confederate River Batteries, and features the "Widow Blakely," the only artillery piece that can be identified as having participated in the siege of Vicksburg. On leaving Louisiana Circle, bear right and drive south onto Washington Street (US 61 and US 80 Business) one-quarter mile to

South Fort, southern anchor of the Confederate defense line and River Batteries line; then continue another quarter-mile to Navy Circle (wartime U.S. Battery Benton), just north of the old bridge over the Mississippi. The total distance from the park Visitor Center to Battery Benton is 4 miles.

Grant's Canal

Union forces under the command of Brig. Gen. Thomas Williams began work on this canal in the summer of 1862 in hope of bypassing the batteries of Vicksburg. Due to intense heat and humidity their efforts were short-lived. Work on the canal was resumed in the winter of 1862-1863 as Maj. Gen. Ulysses S. Grant initiated efforts to capture Vicksburg. The canal efforts were a failure.

Pemberton's Headquarters

Located on Crawford Street in the heart of Vicksburg's historic district this building served as the military headquarters for Confederate Lt. Gen. John C. Pemberton and is where the decision was made to surrender the city on July 4, 1863.

Welcome to Vicksburg

Park Headquarters and Visitor Center are located off Clay Street (US 80, Historic) near Exit 4B, I-20. Exhibits illustrate aspects of the campaign and siege. A 20-minute film dramatizes the decisive phase of operations leading to the surrender of Vicksburg. Information and literature are available. A 16-mile self-guiding tour begins at the Memorial Arch (which commemorates the 1917 reunion of veterans who fought at Vicksburg) and follows a clearly marked route which is adapted for one-way traffic most of the distance. The points of interest starting on page 86, are presented in the order in which you will encounter them on your tour of the battlefield and are keyed to the map inside the back cover.

How to Reach the Park
The park forms an arc behind the business area of Vicksburg, which is served by I-20, US 61, and US 80. Exit 4B of I-20 provides access to the main entrance, located on Clay Street (US 80 Historic) several miles from the Mississippi River.

Administration
The park is administered by the National Park Service, U.S. Department of the Interior. Communications should be addressed to the Superintendent, Vicksburg National Military Park, 3201 Clay Street, Vicksburg, MS 39183-3495. Telephone 601-636-0583. Visit our website **www.nps.gov/vick/**

Related Areas
Other Civil War battlefields administered by the National Park Service and significant to military operations in the West are Shiloh National Military, Fort Donelson National Battlefield, and Stones River National Battlefield, Tennessee; Chickamauga and Chattanooga National Military Park, Georgia-Tennessee; Tupelo National Battlefield and Brices Cross Roads National Battlefield Site, Mississippi; Wilson's Creek National Battlefield, Missouri, and Pea Ridge National Military Park, Arkansas.

Vicksburg, Mississippi, is situated on high bluffs commanding a mighty bend of the Mississippi River, a position of great military and economic importance to both Union and Confederate governments at the beginning of the Civil War.

David G. Farragut's gunboats failed to take the city in the summer of 1862, Gen. Ulysses S. Grant brought his Army of the Tennessee south from Memphis, but all his early efforts failed to subdue the Confederacy's mighty river bastion.

For 14 months the city's defenders successfully turned back every Federal threat to its security, finally succumbing only when the rigors of a 47-day siege by large land and naval forces under Gen. Ulysses S. Grant ultimately proved overwhelming.

The ironclad river gunboat *Cairo*, went down in the Yazoo River on December 12, 1862, the first vessel in naval history to be sunk by an electrically detonated mine. Raised from her watery grave, *Cairo* was brought to the park in 1977 and has been partially restored.

Sixteen miles of roads provide access to nearly 2,000 acres of park land featuring restored forts, rifle-pits, and battery positions, 150 artillery pieces, and more than 1,350 monuments, markers, tablets, busts, relief portraits, and State memorials.

Text and Illustrations are from the Official Vicksburg National Park Handbook. The narrative is derived from an earlier work by William C. Everhart, onetime historian at Vicksburg National Military Park. Photos by Virginia DuBowy. Special thanks to Terry Winschel. Edited & Published by Historic Print & Map Company, St. Augustine, Florida. Designed by Henry Hird III
©2010 Historic Print & Map Company   www.historicprint.com   Printed in the USA   ISBN 978-0-9729463-1-5

The Last Stronghold

Across the imperishable canvas of the American Civil War are vividly recorded feats of arms and armies and acts of courage and steadfast devotion now part of a treasured heritage for all Americans. Among the military campaigns, few, if any, present action of such singular diversity over so vast an area and so consequential to the outcome of the war as the great struggle for control of the Mississippi River. Seagoing men-of-war and ironclad gunboats engaged shore defenses and escorted troops along rivers and bayous; cavalry raids struck far behind enemy lines; and powerful armies marched and countermarched in a gigantic operation which culminated in the siege and capture of Vicksburg.

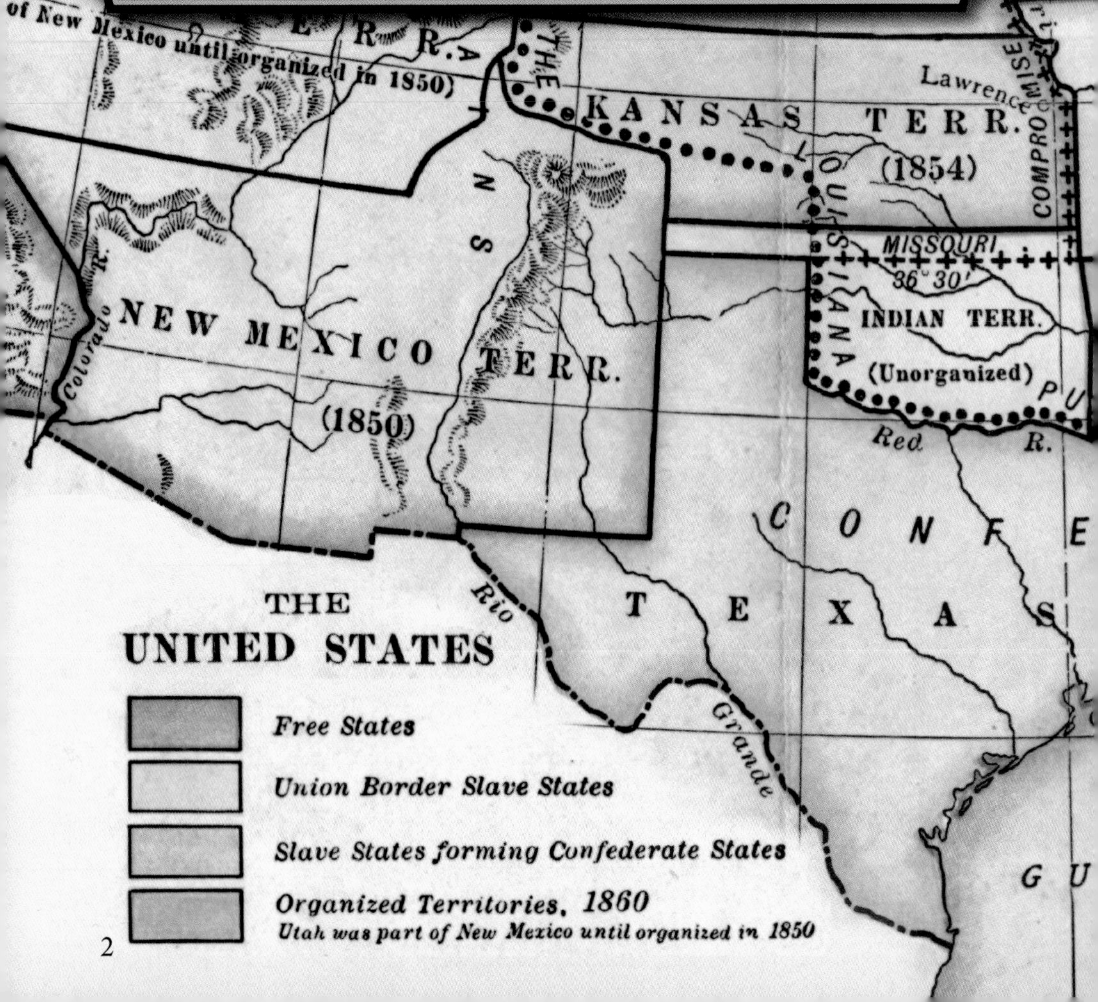

of New Mexico until organized in 1850)
KANSAS TERR. (1854)
Lawrence
COMPROMISE
LOUISIANA
MISSOURI
36° 30'
INDIAN TERR. (Unorganized)
NEW MEXICO TERR. (1850)
Colorado R.
Red R.
Rio Grande
TEXAS
CONFE
THE UNITED STATES
Free States
Union Border Slave States
Slave States forming Confederate States
Organized Territories, 1860
Utah was part of New Mexico until organized in 1850

Opening the lower Mississippi River was a matter of vital concern to the Federal government from the outbreak of hostilities. Union control of this great commercial artery. The course of which meandered more than a thousand miles from Cairo, Illinois, to the Gulf of Mexico, would afford uninterrupted passage for the agricultural and industrial products of the Northwest to markets in New Orleans and beyond. It would also provide an avenue for transporting troops and supplies through a region with few roads and railroads. Moreover, the numerous navigable streams tributary to the Mississippi offered ready routes of invasion into the heart of the South. With this would come the opportunity to cut off and isolate Texas, Arkansas, the Indian Territory, and most of Louisiana, together making up nearly half the land area of the Confederacy and important sources of food, military supplies, and recruits

LAKE SUPERIOR

WISCONSIN

MICHIGAN

LAKE MICHIGAN

LAKE HURON

MICHIGAN

L. ONTARIO

Buffalo

NEW YORK

L. ERIE

ST. Lawrence

MAINE

VERMONT

NEW HAMPSHIRE

MASS.

Boston

CONN.

R.I.

New York

Chicago

ILLINOIS

INDIANA

OHIO

Cincinnati
R.

PENNSYLVANIA

Gettysburg

Antietam

Baltimore

NEW
JERSEY

Philadelphia

DELAWARE

MARYLAND

Washington

Harper's Ferry

Potomac R.

Bull Run

Fredericksburg

Richmond

St. Louis

OURI

Ohio
R.

Louisville

KENTUCKY

Cumberland R.

VIRGINIA

Appomattox o

UNITED STATES

Ft. Donelson

TENNESSEE

Chattanooga

Tennessee
R.

APPALACHIAN

NORTH
CAROLINA

Wilmington

NSAS

Mississippi R.

MISSISSIPPI

Atlanta

ALABAMA

Montgomery

GEORGIA

Savannah R.

SOUTH
CAROLINA

Charleston

Savannah

★ Vicksburg

LOUISIANA

Mobile

FLORIDA

New Orleans

OF   MEXICO

ATLANTIC   OCEAN

BAHAMA
ISLANDS

3